IN THE LIGHT OF GOD'S LOVE

Ty Gibson

Pacific Press® Publishing Association
Nampa, Idaho
Oshawa, Ontario, Canada

Cover design by Matthew McVane
Cover photograph by Tom and Pat Leeson
Design by Matthew McVane

Gibson, Ty, 1963-
    In the light of God's love : a look at the Christian
life / Ty Gibson.
        p.   cm.
    ISBN 13: 978-0-8163-1334-1
    ISBN 10: 0-8163-1334-2 (pbk. : alk. paper)
    1. God's—Love.   2.   God—Worship and love.
3. Love—Religious aspects—Christianity.   4. Christian life—Seventh-day Adventist authors.
    I. Title.
    BT140.G52   1996
    248.4'86732—dc20   96-14451
                                                    CIP

08 09 10 11 • 8 7 6 5

Contents

For Sue
Because of you the love
of Jesus is real to me.

Written to the
inspired and inspiring
music of Johan Sebastian Bach.

First Thoughts

After fourteen years in the church, beginning with a teenager's perspective and moving into full-blown adulthood Adventism, I have assessed our situation and come to a conclusion:

The primary cause of our spiritual weakness is that we have isolated and emphasized vital points of doctrinal truth outside of the context of God's love as manifested at the cross.

Hear me out.

The apostle Paul explained that truth has the power to produce either spiritual death or spiritual life, depending on how we perceive and receive it.

He said it like this:

"The letter killeth, but the Spirit giveth life" (2 Corinthians 3:6).

The letter in Paul's understanding is Bible truth void of Christ. When we intellectually assent to the doctrines of Scripture while simultaneously failing to give focused attention to the person and character of Christ, we come under the death-dealing influence of the *letter* of truth.

To illustrate his meaning Paul points to the Jews as an example of how people are spiritually slain by the letter of truth:

"Their minds were blinded: for until this day remaineth the same veil untaken away in the reading of the old testament; which veil is done away in Christ. But even unto this day, when Moses is read, the veil is upon their heart. Nevertheless when it shall turn to the

Lord, the veil shall be taken away" (2 Corinthians 3:14-16).

They read the Scriptures, Paul says, but their minds were blinded by the very knowledge that should have illuminated them. Intellectually aware of what the prophets said, they were spiritually unenlightened as to what the prophets meant. The biddings and forbiddings of the Bible they had memorized, but the true character of Jehovah woven throughout the Word they did not discern. It was their well-studied purpose to take careful notice of the requirements and threatenings of the Scriptures and then vow with self-righteous determination to obey every command of the Lord; and, I might add, to make sure everyone else did so as well. A veil was upon their hearts, Paul explains, a veil of spiritual blindness that prevented them from understanding the true meaning of the truth of which they boasted.

Of course there is nothing wrong with religious zeal of itself. Their gusto is to be commended. But along with all their big promises to God they cherished one fatal misconception of His character, a misconception so lethal it would eventually work their ruin: They believed that Jehovah's favor and salvation were to be secured by virtue of their knowledge of and obedience to the letter of the law.

This one falsehood corrupted their motives, robbed their hearts of love, and made them powerless to attain the righteousness they tried so desperately to manufacture. Theirs was a pseudo obedience void of joy and rendered under a burden of self-centered fear. They were spiritually dead, while pointing to their doctrines and deeds as evidence that they were alive, slain by the very truths that were intended to give them life.

How could they know so much and yet in reality know so little?

Paul unravels the mystery of their darkened wisdom by drawing a contrast between the letter of truth versus its underlying spirit. While they knew the theory of truth and its outward requirements, they did not understand the true nature of divine love which is the essential element that invests all truth with life-giving power. They did not discern the true spirit of the law, which is love. Consequently, when the personification of the law interrupted their grand masquerade, they crucified Him.

Now before we stretch our necks a few vertebrae higher and mutter, "Yeah, those Jews—*they* were so deceived and self-righteous," perhaps we should consider an enlightened opinion about our own condition as a people:

"We have not held up before the people the righteousness of Christ and the full significance of His great plan of redemption. We have left out Christ and His matchless love, brought in theories and reasonings, and preached argumentative discourses. . . . The law of God has been largely dwelt upon and has been presented to congregations, almost as destitute of the knowledge of Jesus Christ and His relation to the Law as was the offering of Cain" (*Faith and Works*, pp. 16, 18).

The problem of the ancient Jews is our own. They merely acted out as a nation the tendencies of every fallen human heart

- to seek salvation by virtue of personal goodness,
- to emphasize what we can do and de-emphasize what God has done and can do through Christ,
- to find personal glory in our preaching of and

obedience to the letter of truth while passing over its deeper spiritual purpose to transform our characters into the image of divine love.

The remedy for the spiritual blindness of the Jews is set forth by Paul in these simple words:

"The veil is taken away in Christ" (NKJV).

If they had turned to Jesus they would have discerned in Him—in His life, in His teachings, in His sacrifice—the true character of God and the quality of life He desires for all His children.

Our need is the same: Not to merely try and reform our outward lives, nor to put forth greater efforts to proclaim our distinctive doctrines, as important as these things are, but to behold and proclaim God's great love as demonstrated in the life and death of Christ. Then reformation will come to our people, from hearts filled with joyful desire to please and glorify the Lord in all things. Then the distinctive truths of the Remnant Church will be proclaimed to the world, not as mere doctrinal facts, but as shining spotlights that illuminate the character of God.

It is to help hasten that day that this book is published. May we soon come to see and uplift Jesus is my prayer.

1

The Secret Spring of Spiritual Power

❧

"Love is power. Intellectual and moral strength are involved in this principle, and cannot be separated from it. . . . Love cannot live without action, and every act increases, strengthens, and extends it. Love will gain the victory."

Testimonies, vol. 2, p. 135.

ecrets are for sharing. Especially divine secrets—the kind that will increase the strength and joy of fellow travelers in their spiritual journey.

I'd like to whisper into your heart a precious heavenly secret that has touched every aspect of my life with its healing, empowering influence. I call it a secret, not because God has hidden it from us or made it difficult to understand, but because some people won't hear it even if it's shouted, while others will hear it as the faintest whisper.

Why?

Simply because some people want to hear it and some don't.

Maybe you've already heard it and are abiding under its uplifting influence. Or perhaps you've only given it passing notice rather than the priority status it deserves. And then there's the possibility that you have never heard it at all. Whatever may be the case, I am eager to share this life-changing secret with you.

Are you ready? It's profoundly simple, but here it is:

Love is Power.

I told you it was simple. And so it is, but pregnant

with transforming potential. So before you pass it by too lightly, allow me a few paragraphs to enlarge the thought.

I realize that much of what passes for love in our world doesn't deserve more than a passing glance, if even that. For many, love is only an occasional flight of strong sentimental feeling. In many people's vocabulary love is merely a synonym for sex. But I'm talking about something entirely different. Not sentimental love. Not sensual love. But divine love—that love which is the sum and substance of who God is in character.

"God is love," proclaims the Scriptures (1 John 4:16). Love is the actuating principle that gives purpose to every other attribute of God's nature. It determines the selfless quality of His every deed. This love is, as well, the only influence through which we humans are able to experience the truest reality of God's presence in our lives. The apostle John continues: "He who abides in love abides in God, and God in him" (1 John 4:16, NKJV).

John does not say that love is *one of* the good things about God, but that "God *is* love." Neither does he say that *part of* our relationship to God is to experience His love, but that "He who abides in love abides in God, and God in him." Love is the chief attribute of God's character, the totality of the divine identity. And the inflowing and practical outworking of this love is the highest manifestation of God's power in human experience. Abiding in God's love is the real essence of Christian life.

God's love is revealed in many different ways, through various mediums, and in varying degrees.

Through nature. In the providences of our everyday lives. In the human relationships we cherish. But in our present quest to understand divine love I want to move right to its apex manifestation. Hear with your heart these almost unbelievable words of the apostle John:

"In this the love of God was manifested toward us, that God has sent His only begotten Son into the world, that we might live through Him. In this is love, not that we loved God, but that He loved us and sent His Son to be the propitiation [a source of mercy] for our sins" (1 John 4:9, 10, NKJV, words in brackets supplied).

What does it mean?

In the heart of God there exists a quality and depth of love so utterly selfless, and so completely devoted to our happiness and well-being, that He counted our lives more dear than His own. This love found its ultimate expression in the unpretended sacrifice of Jesus Christ, the divine Son of the infinite God. The nature of the sacrifice defines the nature of His love. Consider it with me.

When Jesus became a man He laid aside His equality with God (see Philippians 2:6), which included His omniscience, which is the power to know everything. He couldn't sit under a tree and reminisce about life in heaven before His incarnation. Nor could He see what lay ahead in His future, except by the same means any human being can know the future—by faith in the Word of God.

This is why, when Jesus said with confidence He would be raised from the dead, He concluded the prophecy by saying, "This commandment have I received of My Father" (John 10:18). For Jesus, His resurrection was a matter of faith in God's promise, just as we look forward by faith to our own resurrection should we die before our Lord's return. Under the light of His Father's love and acceptance, He looked forward to life beyond the grave.

But when Jesus entered the Garden of Gethsemane, He began to enter into an entirely new relation to God, unlike the relationship He had enjoyed as the beloved Son in whom the Father was well pleased. Now He felt the shadows of an approaching darkness settling upon Him—so dark, so black, so deep that He felt the sacrifice of His life must be eternal. He was now standing before God as if He were guilty of every sin ever committed by human beings. Jesus, the beloved Son, became a cursed sinner in our place.

As the Sinless Sinbearer, He staggered to the heart of that garden of infinite woe. The disciples were visibly troubled by His changed countenance and heavy step. Jesus broke the silence with this explanation: "My soul is exceedingly sorrowful, even to death" (Matthew 26:38).

The Savior was struggling with a *kind of death* unlike what any human being has ever known—a death that preys upon the soul before it steals life from the body. He was dying at the heart-level of His being before even the first hand had been lifted to torture His flesh. No whip upon His back, no thorns upon His head, no nails through His hands and feet—just a mysterious statement about a death whose sting is lethal sorrow. The Scriptures imply that had not an angel appeared to strengthen Him, He would have died there in the garden before reaching the cross (see Luke 22:43).

Isaiah opens our understanding to what was happening in the Redeemer's heart: "He was wounded [literally, tormented] for our transgressions, He was bruised [crushed] for our iniquities . . . the Lord [God the Father] hath laid on Him [the Son] the iniquity of us all . . . oppressed . . . afflicted . . . cut off . . . for the transgressions of My people . . . His soul an offering for sin . . . He shall bear their iniquities" (Isaiah 53: 5-8, 10, 11; words in brackets supplied).

Paul adds: "For He [the Father] made Him [the Son] who knew no sin to be sin for us" (2 Corinthians 5:21, NKJV; words in brackets supplied).

Jesus took into Himself the guilt of every lie, every theft, every murder, every rape, every sin ever committed by human beings. Consequently, He began to sense in the depths of His inmost heart the separation that sin will ultimately make between God and lost sinners. It was the horror of this reality that caused our destiny to hang in the balance against His own will to continue living in the light of God's love. Three times the tortured will of God's Son was pressed to choose between His own eternal life and ours. "O My Father," He sobbed, "if it is possible, let this cup pass from Me; nevertheless, not as I will, but as You will" (Matthew 26:39, NKJV). Three times He consented to any destiny for Himself, however bleak, in exchange for our redemption.

In Gethsemane the Savior's decision was made to save us at any cost to Himself. At Calvary that choice of love was tested to the utmost. The darkness that only cast its hellish shadow upon Him in the garden now enveloped His soul with the impenetrable blackness of eternal midnight. The Father's love, His acceptance and His approval, seemed so far away as to never return. As Jesus hung there on the cross, the One whose presence alone is life seemed gone forever. The accumulated guilt and shame of the fallen race flooded His heart and hid the Father's face. Sharp with eternal damnation, the sword of divine justice was unsheathed and driven through the innocent heart of the Savior.

"Awake, O sword, against My Shepherd," grieved the Father, "against the Man who is My Companion" (Zechariah 13:7, NKJV).

"Jesus cried out with a loud voice, saying, . . . 'My God, My God, why have You forsaken Me?'" (Matthew 27:46, NKJV).

Forsaken!

What a horrible thought. The word carries the meaning of abandonment, rejection, separation, not for a time, but for *eternity*.

Peering deeper into the mystery of our Savior's sacrifice, Psalm 88 makes an astonishing revelation of what transpired in His agonizing heart: "Thou [Father] hast laid Me [the Son] in the lowest pit, in darkness, in the deeps. Thy wrath lieth hard upon Me. . . . I am shut up and I cannot come forth . . . in the land of forgetfulness" (Psalm 88:6-8, 12; words in brackets supplied). "I am confined and cannot escape . . . in the land of oblivion" (NIV).

Jesus felt with unbuffered force the complete severing of the soul from the love and life of God that sin ultimately causes. Confined in the dungeon of guilt, plunged into the depths of shame, oppressed under the hopeless feelings of never ending separation from God, Jesus endured the full and final wages of sin. He was shut up in the darkness of a death from which He could see no return. And yet He did not relent.

But wait. How could it be? He was the Almighty One. He could have escaped at any moment by a simple act of His omnipotent will, by a single word, even by a thought.

Yes. And here, dear friend, is the wonder of it all. Listen to His incredible claim: "No man taketh it [My life] from Me," He declared, "but I lay it down of Myself" (John 10:18).

Jesus did not endure the cross as a sinner possessed of personal guilt, but as the Savior bearing *by choice* your sin and mine. Had His love for you and me turned out to be secondary to self-interest, in that moment of sinking anguish He could have destroyed the mocking crowd and taken flight back to heaven. Had His love for sinners crumbled under the fear of eternal death, He could have called ten thousand angels to deliver Him. But no, *He chose* to count your life and mine more dear than His own. Compelled by an unconquerable love that knows no bounds, Jesus was willing to cease living forever rather than to seal our doom.

In the realization of such amazing love, do you begin to see that herein, indeed, is a reservoir of untapped spiritual power?

As you contemplate His unreserved sacrifice made for your salvation, do you sense in your heart the inflowing of divine strength, the arousing of moral energy? Do you feel your soul reaching out after Him in willing self-abandonment? I do. When I understand God's matchless love, the things of this world grow strangely dim. Sin looses its attraction. Doubts flee. Troubles become light. Duty becomes a delight. Sacrifice is a pleasure.

Seventeen

That's power, my friend, real power.

Divine love. Unconditional love. Selfless love. Love that soars beyond comprehension. Love that would not let us go. The love of God in Christ. This is the secret spring from which flows all spiritual power. For it captivates the deepest affections of the heart, wins the highest loyalty of the soul, and calls forth the truest praise of the spirit.

No wonder the apostle Paul proclaimed: "The message of the cross is . . . the power of God" (1 Corinthians 1:18, NKJV). For at the cross "God demonstrates His own love toward us" (Romans 5:8, NKJV).

Do you see?

Love is power!

Please do share the secret.

My Father, I am won to Your kingdom by the cross. Your love transcends all this world has to offer. To think that Jesus counted my life more dear than His own! The thought is too high for me. I am eternally Yours. May I never cease to wonder at Your goodness toward me. Thank You! In the precious name of Jesus I pray. Amen.

2

. . . .

Truth

In the Light
of God's Love

❦

"The contemplation of the love of God manifested in His Son will stir the heart and arouse the powers of the soul as nothing else can."

"Nothing reaches so fully down to the deepest motives of conduct as a sense of the pardoning love of Christ."

The Desire of Ages, pp. 478; 493.

I had just finished preaching a sermon on the amazing love of God as demonstrated through Christ at Calvary. A fellowship meal had been planned and small groups of people were visiting while a few of the ladies made the last minute preparations.

As I chatted with a man and his wife I could sense that he was a bit troubled. Something seemed to be on his mind. So I wasn't surprised when, all of a sudden, a surge of boldness came over him.

"What's all this talk about the love of God and the cross? What we need to hear is the *truth!*"

While I halfway expected him to say something negative, I was definitely set back for a few seconds by the nature of his concern.

"The truth?" I questioned. "What is *the truth* you're referring to?"

"You know, *the truth—*" he responded rather matter-of-factly, "the three angels' messages, the mark of the beast, an update on what the pope's up to, the commandments of God, the shaking of the church, the close of probation—*the truth*."

On another occasion while preaching the same

message at one of our universities, an intense man engaged me with a similar line of reasoning.

"You've missed the point," he challenged me. "You're going to lead our people to look lightly on sin with all this emphasis on God's love and the cross. Our church has a real problem and it needs to be fixed."

"Tell me," I probed for his meaning, "in your opinion what is our problem and what is the solution?"

"I'll tell you: The problem is sin, and the solution is we need to stop it. Our people need to hear the *truth*. They need to hear sermons that rebuke their sins, and messages on the commandments of God and standards of the church. That's how we'll check this tide of liberalism coming into the church."

According to these fellows, it is *the truth* we need to be preaching and not the gospel of God's great love manifested in Christ. Quite frankly, I've decided this concept is too deep for me to comprehend. It seems these men are afraid that proclaiming the love of God will not make people feel *obligated enough* to overcome sin and keep His law. And I'm afraid that too many people share their misconception.

The fact is, every doctrinal, prophetic, and lifestyle *truth* of the Bible finds its real value and crucial meaning only in the light of divine love that shines from the cross. Only "the truth as it is *in Jesus*" has power to truly save and sanctify. This is why Paul said, "I determined not to know anything among you, save Jesus Christ, and Him crucified" (1 Corinthians 2:2). The apostle did not mean that he would never address any other topic, but that he would present every other topic in the illuminating context of the cross. He would maintain God's great sacrificial love as the central theme of his ministry. Every other truth of Scripture is invested with power only when kept in vital relation to the knowledge of God's true character as revealed at Calvary.

When doctrinal truths, prophetic truths, or lifestyle truths are presented outside the context of the gospel, the effect is not salvation but rather self-righteousness for some and despair for others.

Doctrine is irrelevant apart from Christ's love.

Prophecy is scary apart from His love.

Lifestyle standards are oppressive apart from His love.

When we point out the difference between right and wrong, individual guilt is accentuated. This is why Paul said, "By the law is the knowledge of sin" (Romans 3:20). We are awakened in conscience to our true condition when the law is presented. And this is just as it should be. The law is intended to occupy that role, and we ought to preach it to accomplish that purpose. But if at this point we fail to magnify God's great love in Christ for the pardon of sin, we risk communicating one of two false impressions with equally devastating results.

False Impression Number One: "I need to keep the law in order to gain the favor and salvation of God."

With this subtle misuse of the law, obedience, standards of holiness, preparation for the close of probation are all perceived as human responsibilities to be borne faithfully in order to secure salvation. Those who tend to be strong-willed and self-confident fall prey to this kind of thinking most easily. Self-righteousness is the result.

False Impression Number Two: "I am utterly hopeless and may as well give up."

Obedience to the law and Christian standards are perceived as obstacles in the way of salvation. The weak and self-conscious fall here. Despair is the result.

But now consider with me the vital part God intends that His love should occupy in the plan of salvation. I think you'll see that it is not risky to focus on the cross. An emphasis on God's love does not give license to sin or cause people to lower standards.

According to the apostle Paul, "The message of the cross *is* the power of God" (1 Corinthians 1:18, NKJV). He enlarges the thought by informing us that the message of the cross is God's love: *"God demonstrates His own love* toward us, in that while we were still sinners, Christ died for us" (Romans 5:8, NKJV). But do not misunderstand Paul's intent. He speaks of God's love, not as a sentimental feeling that makes sinners feel comfortable in their sins, but as a motivating power that enables us to truly be free from sin. In Paul's understanding the love of Christ is the empowering factor in Christian experience.

Notice his words: "The love of Christ constraineth us . . ." (2 Corinthians 5:14). "Christ's love compels us . . ." (NIV). The idea conveyed in this Scripture is motivational power. The love of Christ moves our sin-weakened wills to do things we would never be able to do apart from its animating influence. This is just the kind of power we need, because the Christian life involves various actions of the will that require more than human strength:

• *Repentance*, which is a sorrow for sin so deep that it causes the sinner to turn from his sin.

• *Confession*, which is a humble acknowledgment of personal sin before the Lord.

• *Reformation*, which involves some radical changes of thought, feeling and lifestyle.

All of these aspects of Christian experience are summarized in the penetrating words of Jesus, "Whosoever will come after Me, let him *deny himself*, and take up his cross, and follow Me" (Mark 8:34). Every movement toward God is a movement away from self. The victories to which God calls us and all the changes He requires are, at foundation level, a denial of the old carnal self.

Some undertake this battle in their own strength, supposing that victory over sin and obedience to God's law will come by trying hard enough. So they try, and they tell themselves they're doing pretty good. Others view the task as an insurmountable hurdle beyond the realm of possibility. Eventually they give up in discouragement. In both cases the vital missing element is the motivating, empowering, compelling influence of divine love. What electricity is to a lamp, what fuel is to a car, God's love is to the Christian life.

"The love of Christ constrains" those who receive it, Paul said. To do what? He continues his thought: to "live no longer for themselves, but for Him who died for them and rose again" (2 Corinthians 5:14, 15, NKJV). In other words, the love of Christ is so powerful, so attractive, so absolutely captivating that it moves the one who receives it to cease living for self and to begin living for the One whose love compelled Him to die for us.

When we truly understand and embrace the love of God as illuminated by Calvary, a responsive love awakens deep within our hearts. New desires are stimulated. Personal salvation becomes secondary to His glory. The passion to live for God is made true and deep and strong. Self is forgotten. Christian standards are seen to be Christian privileges. And I might add, for the sake of those who may be worried about all this emphasis on God's love, the very last thing we'll want to do is look lightly on sin.

Everything appears new and beautiful in the light of God's love.

Dear God, cause me to see the true power of Your love. May I not underestimate its transforming influence. Allow the cross to shine its healing rays on my heart so I can view everything in the light of Your love. In Christ's saving name I pray. Amen.

3

Seeing God

In the Light
of His Love

"It is the darkness of misapprehension of God that is enshrouding the world. Men are losing their knowledge of His character. It has been misunderstood and misinterpreted. At this time a message from God is to be proclaimed, a message illuminating in its influence and saving in its power. His character is to be made known. Into the darkness of the world is to be shed the light of His glory, the light of His goodness, mercy and truth. . . . The last rays of merciful light, the last message of mercy to be given to the world, is the revelation of His character of love."

Christ's Object Lessons, p. 415.

ince I travel a lot to conduct revival seminars and evangelistic meetings, I have sometimes encountered expressions of surprise on the faces of people who had formed a picture of me in their minds. Some have vocalized their expectations:

"I thought you would be older."

"I thought you would be taller."

"I thought you would be more solemn looking."

No one has ever told me I looked exactly like they had imagined. (I hope the disappointments have been few.) In more recent years seminar advertisements have included a photo of the speaker. It is so much easier now to get picked up at the airport. My host or hostess knows exactly which face is mine amid the crowd departing the plane.

The fact is, without a photo, it is virtually impossible to form an accurate picture of a person we have never seen. And yet we attempt to do it all the time. We can't help ourselves. We automatically construct mental pictures of people we have never met. Not only do we form pictures of what we think they might look like, we also develop ideas about their personalities.

We are often surprised to discover a person is different than we had expected.

We do the same thing with God. From what we hear other people say about Him, and from our personal experiences in life, we form a picture in our minds of what we think God is like. Many people hold in their minds a picture of God that keeps them from approaching Him. They hate the God they see. Others have developed a view of God that leads them to serve Him like slaves. They are afraid of the God they see. Then there are some who relate to Him as a friend. They must see a beautiful picture of God.

A photo of the Lord would be helpful, don't you think? Then we wouldn't have to guess or go by what others say about Him. Well, believe it or not, God has sent us a photo of Himself. It's not a photo of His face, however. It's a picture of His character:

"For God, who commanded the light to shine out of darkness, hath shined in our hearts, to give the light of the knowledge of the glory of God in the face of Jesus Christ" (2 Corinthians 4:6).

There it is. God's self-portrait has been given to the world in the person of Jesus Christ. We need not depend on our misguided imaginations to know God's character. All we need to do is behold Jesus. By looking at His life, listening to His teachings, and acquainting ourselves with how He related to people, we can form a right conception of our heavenly Father.

Jesus claimed to be the transparent medium through which God is made known. As His earthly ministry was drawing to a close, Philip made a request on behalf of all the disciples: "Show us the Father" (John 14:8, NKJV). No doubt, they wanted to see God in person. Actually, they had, but didn't realize it. Jesus responded, "He who has seen Me has seen the Father" (verse 9).

Jesus could have said it this way: "Do you see how I live, how I care, how I heal, how I love? This is what God is like. I am the living personification, the unobstructed channel, the mirror reflection of God's true character."

Paul called Jesus "the brightness of His [God's] glory, and the express image of His person" (Hebrews 1:3). "Great is the mystery of godliness," he proclaimed, "God was manifest in the flesh" (1 Timothy 3:16).

Jesus was not *kind of* like God, or like God in *some* respects. He was, in the fullest sense, the exact representation of the divine likeness. Every attribute of His character revealed the true personage of God. Every interaction He had with people was a manifestation of the Father's heart. Every episode of His earthly life proclaimed the thoughts and feelings of the Eternal One, whose very nature is love.

At the time of Christ's incarnation the religious leaders had painted a distorted, ugly picture of God. It would have been nice if they had kept it to themselves, but they didn't. With great zeal they held up before the world their custom-crafted image of God. Because they created an image of God in their own likeness, they were unwitting idolaters. By their teachings and their dealings with their fellow human beings, they led minds to conceive of God as a dictatorial and cruel judge, slow to forgive and quick to punish. Generation after generation, as they multiplied impossible rules as obstacles to God's favor and dealt out their condemnations, they repeated their high claim, "We have one Father, even God" (John 8:41).

Naturally, the people of the world assumed God must be like His professed followers. But Jesus denied their representation of the divine character. The picture they presented looked more like the devil than the God of heaven. "If God were your Father," Jesus said, "ye would love Me: for I proceeded forth and came from God; neither came I of Myself, but He sent Me. . . . Ye are of your father the devil, and the lusts of your father ye will do" (John 8:42, 44). They were truly like their father, but God was not their father as they claimed.

Jesus came to our world to give the true knowledge of God. In every act of mercy He was saying, "This is what God is really like." As He healed the sick, as He befriended sinners, as He took time for children, He was longing for the light of divine love to shine into our hearts and persuade us that God is good. This was His appointed mission.

Yet so few understood. The religious leaders said he was a drunk and a glutton because he sought to love those they hated. Even His own disciples struggled to match up their concept of God with what they encountered in Him. Peter tried to shoo away mothers and children, only to be astonished by the Savior's priority interest in giving them undivided attention. James and John suggested that He burn up a whole city, apparently assuming that He would approve of their plan. To their utter surprise, He identified their spirit as from the evil one and not from God. Over and over, throughout His earthly life, Jesus sought to erase the distorted pictures of God people held in their hearts and repaint the image of divinity with the bright and beautiful colors of selfless love. Every act of His life proclaimed, "This is what God is *really* like."

The apostle John recorded one of the Savior's final prayers before His death. In this petition Jesus asked that we would know the true character of God. Listen as Jesus speaks to His Father: "This is life eternal, that they may *know* You, the only *true* God, and Jesus Christ whom You have sent. I have glorified You on the earth. I have finished the work which You have given Me to do. . . . I have manifested Your name" (John 17:3, 4, 6, NKJV).

Did you notice that Jesus defined eternal life in terms of its substance and quality rather than in terms of its length? Eternal life is, in one sense, to live forever. But Christ did not focus on its duration in His prayer. Eternal life is to know God, He said. In other words, eternal life is a life that derives its quality from a knowledge of the true character of God.

Jesus emphasized our need to know the Father as "*the only true God*." It is possible for us to conceive of God in a false light, attributing to Him characteristics that He does not possess. Jesus knew God as He truly is, and He longed for us to discover the transforming beauty of the Father's love. The work God gave Him to do was to manifest the divine character. According to His own testimony, He succeeded in accomplishing that mission.

After all the healings, the acceptance of sinners, the feeding of the hungry, and all the other acts of love He performed, Jesus went to the cross. At Calvary He gave the crowning revelation of God's character. The sacrifice was equally the Father's as well as the Son's. Paul

Thirty-three

affirms that "God was in Christ, reconciling the world unto Himself" (2 Corinthians 5:19). The Son willingly laid down His life; the Father willingly gave up His Son.

Why did the Father make the sacrifice?

One of the most astounding and touching statements Jesus ever made offers the answer to this question. In prayer He reminded the Father, You "have loved them as You have loved Me" (John 17:23, NKJV). I know this is hard to believe, but it's true. God actually loves you and me *as* He loves the Lord Jesus Christ. This remarkable reality exalts God's love so far beyond human love that we can barely take it in. Think of what it means. If He loves you and me as He loves Jesus, that must mean that His love transcends our sin. His love is not altered because of all the wrong things we have done to Him and to others.

In the affairs of human love, if someone does something we don't like or wrongs us in some way, we tend to back up from them. We withdraw our love and acceptance. But God's heart doesn't work that way. Paul says we have been "foolish, disobedient, deceived, serving various lusts and pleasures, living in malice and envy, hateful and hating one another" (Titus 3:3, NKJV). When we see sin in people, we despise them, although we are guilty ourselves. God looks upon us in our wretched state and draws closer yet. His undying, relentless love is not repelled or shut off by our sinfulness. After describing our fallen condition so graphically, Paul astounds us right in the midst of our shame: "But when the kindness and love of God our Savior toward man appeared, not by works of righteousness which we have done, but according to His mercy He saved us" (Titus 3:4, 5).

God the Father sent Jesus to introduce His character to us. He wants us to know Him through His Son. In Christ the measureless love and unbounded kindness of the divine heart was acted out for all the world to see. We need never again question God's thoughts and feelings toward us. In the unmistakable language of love, the life and death of Jesus proclaim that God is good and loving and kind.

We all hold a portrait of God in our hearts. What is He like according to your picture? Are you drawn to the God you see? Does His love surpass every earthly attraction? Do you find yourself overwhelmed with adoration for Him?

If not, maybe you need to take a closer look at His photo. Perhaps you need to behold anew His beautiful image in the life and death of His Son. For only when you truly see Jesus will you truly see God.

O Lord, I do want to see You as You really are, through Jesus, the transparent medium of Your glory. Impress my heart more and more deeply with the goodness of Your character. Then I will serve You without fear all the days of my life. Thank You for who You are. I pray in the glorious name of Jesus. Amen.

4

Salvation

In the Light
of God's Love

✿

"There is not a point that needs to be dwelt upon more earnestly, repeated more frequently, or established more firmly in the minds of all than the impossibility of fallen man meriting anything by his own best good works. Salvation is through faith in Jesus Christ alone."

Faith and Works, p. 19.

I kind of, sort of, think that maybe I possibly might end up being saved."

If it weren't so serious it would be funny. Tragically, there are many—and I mean *many*—Seventh-day Adventists who feel just that uncertain about their destiny.

How unlike Paul: "God hath not given us the spirit of fear; but of power, and of love, and of a sound mind . . . who hath saved us, and called us with an holy calling, not according to our works, but according to His own purpose and grace, which was given us in Christ Jesus before the world began . . . who hath abolished death, and hath brought life and immortality to light through the gospel . . . I know whom I have believed, and am persuaded that He is able to keep that which I have committed to Him against that day" (2 Timothy 1:7, 9, 10, 12).

How unlike John: "This is the testimony: that God has given us eternal life, and this life is in His Son. He who has the Son has life; he who does not have the Son of God does not have life. . . . You may know that you have eternal life" (1 John 5:11-13, NKJV).

Obviously these men understood something about the plan of salvation that many of us have missed. Their voices ring with such a clear testimony of confidence.

God has saved us, Paul proclaims, *and I know, I believe, I am persuaded that He will keep me.*

God has given me eternal life in His Son, John exalts, *and I know that I have eternal life.*

Then, in stark contrast, listen to our whimpering dirge: "I think . . . I hope . . . It will be nice if I make it. But if I don't, God knows I tried."

What is the problem? What is missing in our thinking?

Well, according to Paul, the "life and immortality" of which he was so confident was "brought to light through the gospel" (2 Timothy 1:10). The gospel is the key. To the church at Thessalonica he said the "gospel came . . . in much assurance" (1 Thessalonians 1:5). It was Paul's understanding of the gospel that gave him such strong assurance of salvation. We can logically assume, then, that our lack of assurance has grown out of a misunderstanding of the gospel.

In this chapter I want to address one basic difference between what many people believe concerning salvation and what the Bible clearly teaches. This single facet of the gospel, if understood, will do much to dispel the dark clouds of doubt that hang over us.

To a large degree our view of the gospel has been shaped by our response to the cheap grace or once-saved-always-saved extreme of some evangelical churches. They have taught that the grace of God makes obedience or good works irrelevant for the Christian. Once you believe in Jesus, you are saved and there is nothing you can do to forfeit eternal life, they might say.

In response to this erroneous view we have argued, in tone if not in words, "No, we are saved by grace through faith *and* good works." Salvation is like a partnership—God does some of the saving and we do some of the saving, we have implied. Our sincerity is shown by *our* obedience, and if we do well enough, then God will give us eternal life.

With this kind of emphasis it is natural for us to look at ourselves to determine our standing with God. And because we look to ourselves, we are never really sure of salvation and we often feel we are not good enough to be saved.

Because these two positions have been in such prominent opposition to one another, many of us have assumed that these are the only two theological options. But there is a third view we should consider. The Biblical one! Let's compare all three:

Option One
Some say we are saved by grace through faith *apart* from good works, which makes obedience *irrelevant*.

Option Two
Some say we are saved by grace through faith *and* good works, which makes obedience *meritorious*.

Option Three
But the Bible teaches that we are saved by grace through faith *unto* good works, which makes obedience *inevitable*.

Notice how carefully and beautifully Paul builds the structure of his theological position on salvation:

"For by grace are ye saved through faith; and that not of yourselves: it is the gift of God: not of works, lest any man should boast. For we are His workmanship, created in Christ Jesus unto good works, which God hath before ordained that we should walk in them" (Ephesians 2:8-10).

Grace is the primary factor by which we are saved. Grace, of course, pertains wholly to God. He alone is its origin. For grace is, in essence, the merciful attitude with which God relates to us in our sin.

Faith is the capacity God has deposited in every human heart to respond to His grace (see Romans 12:3). He is the Author of our faith (see Hebrews 12:2). But while He created our faith and placed it in our hearts, He will not exercise it for us. So in the sense that we are to exercise the faith He has given, it can be said that faith is our part. Even so, He does not leave us to exercise the gift of faith on our own. Not only has He given us faith as a free gift, He also takes upon Himself the responsibility of awakening our faith to action. He does this by drawing our attention to His infinite love as it was manifested at the cross. So Paul says that faith "worketh by love" (Galatians 5:6). That is, faith is made active by encounter with God's love. Love is the motivating factor in the plan of salvation. God's love arouses and moves faith in us to so appreciate His grace that we willingly and joyfully yield to His purpose for our lives.

This is where good works come into the picture. Paul emphatically informs us that our salvation is "not *of* works, lest any man should boast." Language could not be clearer. We are *not* saved in any degree by virtue of works. But that does not conclude Paul's comments about works. In verse 10 he says we are "created in Christ Jesus *unto* good works." So while we are not saved *of*, we are definitely saved *unto* good works. What is the difference? It is the chasm of difference that exists between almost every false religion in the world and the singular gospel of Jesus Christ. Islam, Buddhism, Hinduism, Judaism, and Catholicism all say to fallen humanity, "Do good and God will give you salvation in exchange." The gospel of Christ says to sinners, "God has given you salvation as a free gift in His Son; receive the glad tidings by faith and God will do good in and through you."

I can hear someone responding: "If what you're saying is true, then good works do not precede and are of no value to secure salvation."

I realize this is a seriously humbling idea, but yes, that is exactly what the Bible is saying. Now go ahead and ask the next logical question.

"OK, I will. If we are not saved by our works, why are they even necessary?"

I'm so glad you asked that question. Jesus gives the answer. Listen to Him: "Let your light so shine before men, that they may see your good works, and glorify your Father which is in heaven" (Matthew 5:16). Jesus does not say, *Do good works so you will be saved*. He says, *Do good works so others will encounter the goodness of God in you and glorify Him.*

Isaiah foretold the coming of Christ "to preach good tidings." He said that one effect of the gospel message would be righteousness in the lives of those who believe. Then he pointed out that the righteousness of Christ's followers would have a special purpose. He called them "trees of righteousness, *that He might be glorified*" (Isaiah 61:3).

Paul understood the very same relation between works of righteousness in the believer's life and the glory of God: "Being filled with the fruits of righteousness, which are by Jesus Christ, *unto the glory and praise of God*" (Philippians 1:11). Notice that Paul viewed the righteousness brought forth in the Christian's life as *fruits*. Fruits of what? Of salvation no doubt. In other words, righteousness does not secure salvation, but salvation does produce righteousness. Therefore, Paul says the fruits of righteousness are "*by* Jesus Christ." That is to say, Jesus is the source of the righteousness that will be seen in the Christian life. It is natural, then, in the logical flow of Paul's thoughts for him to connect the righteous living of the believer with the glory of God. Since it is "not by works of righteousness which we have done, but according to His mercy He saved us" (Titus 3:5), all the righteous deeds in our lives are the fruits of His grace and thus the mirror reflection of His glory. So Paul could say without the slightest exaggeration, "For *of* Him, and *through* Him, and *to* Him, are all things: to whom be glory for ever. Amen" (Romans 11:36).

A sinner saved and made righteous by the free grace of God brings glory to the One who has done the saving. It is God's purpose to "make known the riches of His glory on the vessels of mercy" (Romans 9:23). We are those vessels. As objects of extravagant grace, we have nothing of which to boast other than the cross of Jesus Christ. It is to protect us from self-glory that Paul warns us not to attribute any degree of merit to our good works, for if we were "justified by works," we would have "something of which to boast" or "glory" (Romans 4:2, NKJV and KJV).

Now return with me to the basic structure of Paul's salvation theology in Ephesians 2:8-10:

- We are saved
- by grace
- through faith
- not *of* but *unto* good works.

It is vital that we understand the order of the experience. Salvation comes by grace through faith alone. Good works are the practical outworking of that reality. The moment we reverse the inspired order by placing deeds of righteousness before salvation, at least three spiritual tragedies result:

1. The motives of the heart are corrupted, because self becomes the center of our focus rather than Christ.

2. True obedience becomes impossible, because true obedience is the outworking of a heart filled with Christ-centered love, and is not the purchase price of salvation.

3. Joy in obedience becomes impossible, because we only find joy in obedience that is motivated by love.

The true gospel is designed to lay the glory of man in the dust so God can do for us what we cannot do for ourselves. Sure, we can modify our outward behavior so as to give an appearance of righteousness. But only Christ can change us at the heart level.

How does He do it?

By convincing us that there is nothing good we have ever done or can do to secure His salvation. Then, as we lose all confidence in ourselves and almost sink into hopelessness, He graciously informs us that we need not despair, for He has saved us by virtue of His love.

This understanding of the gospel is perfectly calculated to accomplish two revolutions in the human heart: (1) It totally shatters every vestige of self-dependence for salvation and shifts our dependence wholly to Christ, and (2) it awakens in us a depth of gratitude and love that can find satisfaction only in living to please and honor Christ.

Do you see, friend, that anything short of full and free salvation through Christ alone will leave self alive?

Do you see that you can never really live for the Lord until you have the assurance that your salvation rests in Him alone and not in yourself?

Do you see that gratitude to Jesus for a free salvation is more powerful to produce a life of righteousness than is a mere sense of obligation to be good in order to secure salvation. (Read that sentence again, please.)

So what do you believe, my friend? How does Jesus save sinners? Ponder the options carefully, and make no mistake.

1. Salvation by grace through faith *apart* from good works, which makes obedience irrelevant.

2. Salvation by grace through faith *and* good works, which makes obedience meritorious.

3. Or, salvation by grace through faith *unto* good works, which makes obedience inevitable. Inevitable, because God's grace is sufficient. Inevitable, because the faith He gives really does work. Inevitable, because in the light of God's love I willingly and joyfully accept His will as my own. Not so I can be saved, but that He might be glorified in me as the Savior.

SALVATION

I assure you, the way you think concerning this vital matter will determine, more than all other factors combined, the quality of your Christianity—whether your experience will be one of rest or anxiety, confidence or uncertainty, joy or gloom, love or fear, victory or defeat.

Father, I praise You for devising such a perfect plan to save me. There is something in me that wants to take some of the glory for my redemption. But if I believe the gospel, and I do, all things pertaining to my salvation are of You, through You, and to You. That means I can do nothing to save myself, but You have saved me totally by virtue of Your infinite love. It's humbling, but it's also a relief, for deep inside I know I'm a helpless subject of Your grace. Thank You. In the all-sufficient name of Jesus I Pray. Amen.

5

Obedience

In the Light
of God's Love

"There are those who profess to serve God, while they rely upon their own efforts to obey His law, to form a right character, and secure salvation. Their hearts are not moved by any deep sense of the love of Christ, but they seek to perform the duties of the Christian life as that which God requires of them in order to gain heaven. Such religion is worth nothing. When Christ dwells in the heart, the soul will be so filled with His love, with the joy of communion with Him, that it will cleave to Him; and in the contemplation of Him, self will be forgotten. Love to Christ will be the spring of action."

Steps to Christ, pp. 44, 45.

arriage has the potential to be either the most fulfilling experience two people can have together or the most miserable burden of life. Sad to say, many people mumble a weary *Amen* to the last half of that statement.

What is the factor in marriage that determines the quality of the relationship? Love, of course. If a man and a woman truly love one another their marriage will bring them great satisfaction and joy. If, on the other hand, selfishness is allowed to reign, mutual respect will be lost and the relationship will begin to feel confining. The sacrifices that the relationship requires will become a heavy burden.

Christianity is very much like marriage. It can be either a wonderful experience or a terrible one. And the determining factor is the same. Love.

As in marriage, a relationship with God will call for sacrifices. Marriage requires the submission of each spouse's will to that of the other. Christianity requires the submission of the will to Christ. When the heart is kept truly in love with the Lord, obedience to His will brings great satisfaction and joy. However, if we obey Him merely out of a sense of self-concerned obligation in order to gain heaven, His law will seem restrictive and even oppressive.

There are many who are trying to live by the standards and commandments of God's word because they want to escape hell and gain heaven. Their hearts are not moved by any deep sense of the love of God, but they do realize their guilt and they fear the loss of their souls. So they set their feet in the path of duty and determine to live in harmony with God's will. They hope in this way to be saved. The fact is, they really do not obey the Lord, because the heart is not into the matter. They are not truly willing, but merely feel obligated. They perform the letter of the law, but they are not actuated by the true spirit of obedience, which is love (see 2 Corinthians 3:6 and Romans 13:10).

In the Bible there are two kinds of obedience brought to view. One is referred to by Paul as *the works of the law*, and by Jesus as *outward righteousness*. The other Paul called *obedience from the heart*, or simply *love*. Jesus described it as *inward righteousness* and also summarized it with the single word *love*.

Works of the law are deeds of outward obedience rendered
   • out of a mere sense of obligation in order to be saved,
      • without personal willingness from the heart,
      • without inward delight,
      • without a sincere desire to please God,
      • and with a view of God's character that assumes He withholds His favor until we do good.

Obedience from the heart involves an inward attitude toward God that springs forth

- from a deep sense of God's love in giving His Son to die for our sins,
- from a personal desire to do God's will because it is pleasing to Him,
- with inward delight,
- and with sincere appreciation to God for the free salvation He has given us through Christ apart from any works of righteousness which we have done.

In His sermon on the mount Jesus confronted the people with a startling challenge: "Unless your righteousness exceeds the righteousness of the scribes and Pharisees, you will by no means enter the kingdom of heaven" (Matthew 5:20, NKJV).

This was a serious statement to bear for those who heard Him. As far as they could see the scribes and Pharisees were the perfect example of righteousness. They were as righteous as humans get, the cream of God's crop. Now Jesus was telling them that they needed to be more strict than the most righteous people they knew.

Or was He?

Either Jesus was saying that we need more of the same righteousness the scribes and Pharisees exhibited, or He was inviting us to receive a righteousness of an entirely different character and quality. In Matthew 23 Jesus addressed the scribes and Pharisees with some straight words. On this occasion He clearly pointed out the difference between their righteousness and that to which He was calling the people. Carefully notice His words:

"Woe to you, scribes and Pharisees, hypocrites! For you pay tithe of mint and anise and cumin, and have neglected the weightier matters of the law: justice and mercy and faith. These you ought to have done, without leaving the others undone.

"Blind guides, who strain out a gnat and swallow a camel! Woe to you, scribes and Pharisees, hypocrites! For you cleanse the outside of the cup and dish, but inside they are full of extortion and self-indulgence.

"Blind Pharisees, first cleanse the inside of the cup and dish, that the outside of them may be clean also.

"Woe to you, scribes and Pharisees, hypocrites! For you are like whitewashed tombs which indeed appear beautiful outwardly, but inside are full of dead men's bones and all uncleanness. Even so you also outwardly appear righteous to men, but inside you are full of hypocrisy and lawlessness" (Matthew 23:23-27, NKJV).

According to Jesus we humans are composed of two basic parts—the outside and the inside. Obviously He was referring to our behavioral appearance as the outside, and to our heart-motives as the inside.

The scribes and Pharisees were extremely concerned about the outward issues of religion and at the same time very neglectful of the inward matters. As an example of the outward things on which they were so focused, the Savior mentioned tithing. He could have as easily used Sabbath observance or dietary habits as His example. In contrast to issues of outward conduct, Jesus called their attention to "the weightier matters of the law: justice and mercy and faith," and Luke's gospel adds to the list, "the love of God" (Luke 11:42).

Jesus did not dismiss outward behavior as of no importance, for He said such things should not be left undone. Rather, He was trying to shift their *focus* from the outward to the inward. In God's mind there are *gnat* size issues and there are *camel* size issues. A gnat is very small in comparison to a camel. So there are matters of paramount importance, such as faith and love. Then there are matters of comparatively small significance, such as paying tithe and drinking gnat-free water (dietary habits).

Remember, it is Jesus who has drawn this distinction, not me.

But why any distinction at all?

Jesus came right to the practical point He was leading to: "First cleanse the inside of the cup and dish, that the outside of them may be clean also."

First in point of priority. *First* in point of focus. *First* in point of time. "*First* cleanse the inside," He says.

That. So that. In order that. "*That* the outside may be clean."

Also. In addition to. As an effect of. Coming forth from. "That the outside may be clean *also*."

In other words, focus your attention and energies on the vital matters of the heart, such as faith and love, and as a result the outward matters of reform and conduct will be taken care of in natural course—*from the inside out*.

God's love in us will not fulfill the law superficially, as mere outward conformity to God's rules in order to avert His wrath and secure His favor. When God's love penetrates the heart it creates in the wake of its influence a new spring of action, a new attitude toward God and His law, a new reason to live.

We once lived in the passion of self-interest. Our highest priority was our personal salvation, assuming we could do something about it by performing righteous works. But now, in the light of God's love, we live in the compelling passion of Christ-centered affection. Our highest priority is God's glory, for we realize He saves us totally by virtue of His mercy and not because of any works of righteousness which we have done.

Paul's language is different than that of Jesus, but equally clear: "God be thanked, that ye were the servants of sin, but ye have obeyed *from the heart* that form of doctrine which was delivered you" (Romans 6:17).

What does the apostle mean by this idea of obedience from the heart?

In his own context Paul's understanding is made evident: "Having been justified by faith, we have peace with God through our Lord Jesus Christ, through whom also we have access by faith into this grace in which we stand, and rejoice in hope of the glory of God" (Romans 5:1, 2, NKJV).

The gospel Paul proclaimed was the good news of justification by faith in Jesus Christ alone. He rejoiced in this amazing realization of divine grace. In verse 5 he explains the effect this gospel has on those who believe: "The love of God has been poured into our hearts by the Holy Spirit who was given to us." When the true gospel dawns upon the understanding, the love of God fills the heart with unquenchable desire to please such a wonderful Lord. It is with this gospel in mind that Paul speaks of believers obeying from the heart. He simply means obedience that has its origin in love, springing forth from a heart that has been won and transformed at the motive level.

The apostle John communicated the same idea when he said, "Whoever believes that Jesus is the Christ is born of God, and everyone who loves Him who begot also loves Him who is begotten of Him. . . . This is the love of God, that we keep His commandments. And His commandments are not burdensome" (1 John 5:1, 3, NKJV).

Love is the only source of true obedience, and true obedience is not a burden. In fact, it is the highest blessing the believer knows. The one whose religious experience centers in God's love can identify with David when he said, "I delight to do Thy will, O my God: yea, Thy law is within my heart" (Psalm 40:8). Obedience that comes from the heart is obedience in which there is delight. It is not a pretended or disciplined delight that is put on for others to see. No, it is a personal delight, an inner joy that abides in the heart whether others are looking or not.

Those who do not understand the power of God's love to awaken in the heart a living, working faith, will talk of salvation by faith *and* works. Because they minimize God's love, they must find some human goodness to add to their deficient view in order to make it appear as though their religion is getting the job done. But the Bible knows nothing of a salvation that comes through faith *and* works, but only of a faith that does work . . . by love (see Galatians 5:5, 6).

Salvation is by grace through faith, period. Nothing more. The moment we add anything, there is room for boasting. God's grace is so transforming, and the faith He has given us is so effectual, that every true child of the gospel will be made a masterpiece of good works— no credit to us. Paul does not leave works out of the picture, he simply puts them in their proper place as the fruit of salvation and not the root. He says that salvation is "not *of* works," but definitely "*unto* good works" (Ephesians 2:8-10). In other words, salvation is not secured by good works, but does produce them.

It is only in the consciousness of God's marvelous grace, by which we are freely saved apart from any works, that we truly prevail over sin and obey the Lord. For when we comprehend the love of Christ which surpasses knowledge, we are made entirely new on the inside. Because God's love transforms the springs of motive in the inmost heart, love for sin is conquered as love for God reigns.

In the light of God's love, obedience is a blessing not a burden, a delight not drudgery, a privilege not a problem. The heart that has been impressed with a true sense of God's love will not complain or quibble about the high standards of holiness the Lord holds up. There will be no question as to how little can be done in order to slip into heaven. We will not ask, *What does God require*? with a tone that suggests an interest in minimum requirements. One great passion will reign supreme in the soul—the honor and glory of God.

So turn your eyes away from yourself. Fasten your gaze upon the cross of Christ. Rivet your attention there until the reality of God's astounding love wins the deepest loyalty of your heart.

I think you'll find that Christianity is like marriage. Love makes all the difference in the world.

Loving Father, precious Lord Jesus, grant that I would know the wonderful experience of obedience from the heart. Teach me to find inward delight in Your holy law. Win me, dear Savior, win me at the deepest level of my motives. In Christ I pray. Amen.

6

Dealing With Temptation

In the Light
of God's Love

.

"It is because selfishness exists in our hearts that temptation has power over us. But when we behold the great love of God, selfishness appears to us in its hideous and repulsive character, and we desire to have it expelled from the soul. As the Holy Spirit glorifies Christ, our hearts are softened and subdued, the temptation loses its power, and the grace of Christ transforms the character."

Thoughts from the Mount of Blessing, p. 118.

e's ornery. He's tricky. He's deceitful. He's uncontrollable. He's desperately wicked.

Worst of all, he's *You*!

I don't mean to be hard on you, but someone needs to confront you with the reality of your pitiful condition. Please *do* take it personal. It's God's diagnosis, not only of you, but of me too.

"The heart is deceitful above all things, and desperately wicked: who can know it?" (Jeremiah 17:9).

"Because the carnal mind is enmity against God: for it is not subject to the law of God, neither indeed can be" (Romans 8:7).

Of course, if you've been born again, in addition to the *old* you there is also the *new* you. I guess we could say there are *two* you's. Not that you're schizophrenic, but you do definitely have two persons battling for the mastery in your life.

There are many folks, however, who try to *live* new without *becoming* new. They try to make the old man of sin live the new man lifestyle of righteousness. Though a futile pursuit, nevertheless, scores of undeniably zealous men and women keep on trying to go the do-it-yourself route. They mistakenly suppose God wants them to merely modify and reform the old person that they are. Or perhaps they just don't think about it carefully enough to realize that this is what they're doing.

There are three basic strategies that old-man-Christians use to deal with temptation and attempt to live the victorious life:

1. *Magnified Guilt.* By focusing on their past failures, some people hope to make themselves feel so guilty that they won't feel audacious enough to sin again: "I'm so terrible. I can't believe I did *that.* I'm so low, so depraved, so vile. If I don't get my act together, I'll end up lost for sure. I know I can do better, and I promise I will."

2. *Increased Sense of Duty.* There is a line of complex reasoning designed to increase a sense of duty that goes something like this: "It's wrong and you know it's wrong, so don't do it, because it really is wrong, it's just plain wrong, so don't you dare do it, since it's wrong and you know you shouldn't—even though you want to." (Versions may vary according to personality.)

3. *Brute Strength.* Sometimes when we are trying to be Christians without Christ we come right up to the forbidden deed and stare it straight in its sinful eyes, clinch our fists, grind our teeth and say, "NOOOO! Nooo! No. no. no. . . . oh noooo."

Now don't misunderstand me. When we do wrong, we ought to feel guilty about it. We do need to have a high sense of duty too. And when faced with temptation, we should say No, with furrowed eyebrow if necessary. But listen: None of these approaches will avail to make the old man behave himself. The problem is not just that he doesn't want to be good—he cannot. Good intentions, resolute promises, brute determination are useful for running a business or building a house; but here they are powerless. We need an entirely new heart, not merely a disciplining of the old one. The gospel does not call us to merely try and be good people. Rather, it summons us to die and rise to newness of life.

So what is the new heart and how do we receive it? Here's God's promise:

"I will give you a new heart and put a new spirit within you; I will take the heart of stone out of your flesh and give you a heart of flesh. I will put My Spirit within you and cause you to walk in My statutes, and you will keep My judgments and do them" (Ezekiel 36:26, 27, NKJV).

In the Bible *the heart* is often mentioned with an intended spiritual meaning. The literal, biological heart was seen as the divinely ordained center and source of physical life. So the heart was referred to as a symbol of the central faculties of man's spiritual nature. When used in this way its primary meaning seems to be *the will* or *the motivational mainspring* of human nature.

The word *spirit* has a closely related meaning. The spirit of man was rightly thought to be the breath or life force of God. In a spiritual sense it may be taken to mean the quality of spiritual life one sustains in his or her relation to God. More specifically, it refers to the disposition or attitude toward God.

With this understanding in mind, we might read the above Scripture like this: "I will give you new motivation and put a new quality of life within you; I will take the selfish motives out of you and give you a willing heart that will be soft and pliable, a heart that will incline toward Me. I will put My Holy Spirit within you and will influence you at the level of your motives and in this way cause you to live in harmony with My will."

There are many who try to *be* Christians before they *become* Christians in God's appointed way. They set out on a course to correct bad habits and do righteous deeds, assuming that by so doing they are Christians, but they are beginning in the wrong place. The first work of the Holy Spirit is to change *the heart,* not correct *the life.* The outward life may be disciplined so as to give an appearance of Christianity, while the heart is left untouched. But if the heart is first transformed, the life will reflect that inner reality.

Consider these insightful words:

"As the leaven, when mingled with the meal, works from within outward, so it is by the renewing of the heart that the grace of God works to transform the life. No mere external change is sufficient to bring us into harmony with God. There are may who try to reform by correcting this or that bad habit, and they hope in this way to become Christians, but they are beginning in the wrong place. Our first work is with the heart. . . .

"The man who attempts to keep the commandments of God from a sense of obligation merely—because he is required to do so—will never enter into the joy of obedience. He does not obey. When the requirements of God are accounted a burden because they cut across human inclination, we may know that the life is not a Christian life. True obedience is the outworking of a principle within. It springs from the love of righteousness, the love of the law of God. The essence of all righteousness is loyalty to our Redeemer. This will lead us to do right because it is right—because right doing is pleasing to God" (*Christ's Object Lessons*, pp. 97, 98).

We do not become Christians by overcoming sin. We overcome sin by becoming Christians. And we become Christians by coming to Christ. We must first turn to the cross and receive the new heart before we suppose we are any match for sin. As we comprehend the amazing love of Christ as revealed at Calvary, the old selfish heart will die and the new heart of love will come to life. The hard spirit of stubbornness will give way to a new spirit that inclines toward the Lord with delight.

Receiving the new heart is not some kind of mystical transplant. It simply means a change of motivation. God created Adam with a heart that was governed by the supreme motivation of love to God and love to others. When Adam sinned there was a fundamental change that took place in his nature—selfishness took the place of love. Selfishness became the governing force in his decision making.

When we embrace the revelation of God's love displayed at the cross, selfishness is conquered and the original motivation of love is restored to the heart. This is what it means to be born again. In fact, this is the only real way to become a Christian.

Genuine conversion only happens in the light of the cross, when the soul encounters Calvary's love and yields to its influence. Conversions founded on a platform of unresolved guilt, or on a mere sense of duty, or on brute determination are superficial and will only supply strength proportional to the weakness of the

Sixty-five

foundation. When storm winds of temptation really blow, such religion will be found to be worth nothing. Like a house built on sand, it will be swept away, but those who build on the solid foundation of Christ will stand against the fiercest temptations.

Why?

Not because they feel too guilty to sin.

Not because they feel obligated.

Not because they try hard enough.

But because their loyalties have been so won by divine love that they would rather die than sin against their precious Savior; because God's love is stronger than temptation to sin. It is the most powerful force in all the universe. It is our greatest and most basic need.

Once we have come to Christ and received the new heart, it is by the same means that we are to continue in Him. "As [or in the same way] you have therefore received Christ Jesus the Lord, so walk in Him" (Colossians 2:6, NKJV; words in brackets supplied). As we become born again by the realization of God's love at the foot of the cross, so we are to maintain our new life by remaining under the powerful influence of the cross.

Allow me to explain in more practical terms. Temptation and motivation are very similar concepts. We use the word temptation to describe negative attractions, while we often use the word motivation to refer to positive attractions. When we say we are tempted we mean we feel prompted to do something wrong. When we say we are motivated we usually mean we feel prompted to do something good.

Temptation and motivation are mortal enemies. The first is Satan's primary weapon for the ruin of souls. The second is the Lord's chief advantage for the salvation of souls. We can easily see then that we need to pursue a course of spiritual discovery that will increase the strength of God-ward motivation in our hearts and weaken the influence of temptation to sin.

The apostle Paul explains what our strategy ought to be:

"Let us lay aside every weight, and the sin which so easily ensnares us, and let us run with endurance the race that is set before us, looking unto Jesus, the author and finisher of our faith, who for the joy that was set before Him endured the cross, despising the shame, and has sat down at the right hand of the throne of God" (Hebrews 12:1, 2, NKJV).

Notice the relation between overcoming sin and focusing on Jesus. The first few words of this Scripture express the most significant challenge we face: *Lay aside the sin which so easily ensnares us*. Paul knew that sin strikes a responsive carnal-cord in our hearts. We naturally tend toward sin.

Yes, Paul does say it will take personal endurance to gain the victory, but not endurance of itself. He joins endurance to something else—*looking unto Jesus*. By focusing the heart's affections, sympathies and understanding on the Savior, who endured the cross out of His great love for us, the exercise of the will in dealing with temptation will be made effectual. It is the abiding sense of Christ's love that makes the heart strong to conquer sin.

The concept is simple: The more distant from our thoughts is the cross of Christ, the stronger will be the appeals of temptation. The greater is our conscious appreciation of the cross, the mightier will be the heart's will to vanquish sin.

Or we could say it this way: The more motivated we are by God's love, the less tempted we will be by sin. In the light of God's love, sin loses its attraction and all of God's ways become beautiful in our eyes.

So Paul's basic formula for dealing with temptation is this:

- Lay aside sin,
- with faithful endurance,
- by looking unto Jesus, who endured the cross.

Trying to lay aside sin by personal endurance, of itself, will eventually tucker out even the most self-willed. It is absolutely vital that we combine with our efforts a constant, progressively deepening focus on the life and love and cross of Jesus.

Unless Jesus is made the all in all of our Christian experience, it simply will not work. No matter how sincere we are, no matter how hard we try, we can never live the Christian life apart from Christ. If we don't learn this lesson by the testimony of Scripture, hopefully we will learn it by experience. If not, we will eventually cast Christianity to the wind as an illusive dream. And it won't be because we didn't know the rules, but because we didn't know the One who made the rules.

Yes, Father, I've experienced the futility of trying to deal with temptation in my own strength. I've tried to make myself do right and resist wrong on my own. It's an endless round of failure. I so need the new heart, a heart that moves at the impulse of Your love. As I look to Jesus, who endured the cross for me, please renew that heart in me day by day. In His mighty name I pray. Amen.

7

When I Fall

*In the Light
of God's Love*

"There are those who have known the pardoning love of Christ and who really desire to be children of God, yet they realize that their character is imperfect, their life faulty, and they are ready to doubt whether their hearts have been renewed by the Holy Spirit. To such I would say, Do not draw back in despair. We shall often have to bow down and weep at the feet of Jesus because of our shortcomings and mistakes, but we are not to be discouraged. Even if we are overcome by the enemy, we are not cast off, not forsaken and rejected of God."

Steps to Christ, p. 64.

I will never forget Diane. She was so sweet and yet so discouraged. It was with little hope that she approached me for a solution to her problem. As far as she could see, her Christian experience was at an end with no possible recourse, but her husband urged her to attend one of my seminars and give the Lord another chance. Part way through the series of meetings she asked if she might have a few minutes of my time. I could see she was deeply troubled. Without hesitation I stepped aside with her. This is what she said:

"A few weeks ago I attended a series of meetings. The speaker read certain Scriptures and said that if a person is *truly* converted all sin has been removed from the heart, and the *true* Christian will not sin as long as he remains born-again. If you do sin, that means either you never really were a Christian or you are no longer converted. A truly converted person does not sin."

She continued, "When I heard this I was completely overwhelmed with feelings of despair. In all honesty I could not claim to be a *true* Christian. I had thought that I loved Jesus and that He had accepted me, but now I was certain I had never really been converted.

"Before I came to your meetings I had already decided that Christianity must not be for me. But I know it is the truth, so I determined to keep up the Christian lifestyle for my children's sake. *Even if I can't make it, maybe they can,* I told myself. But what you're presenting is not the same as what I heard in the other seminar. I'm so confused. I don't know if I'm converted or not. Is there any hope for me?"

I must say, I was not surprised by Diane's struggle. Through the years I've met numerous other such prisoners of "King Despair." The theology Diane encountered is not uncommon fare in conservative circles.

"Diane," I inquired, "do you love Jesus with all your heart?"

"Yes . . . well I thought I did, but . . ."

"Save your but's," I stopped her. "Do you love Jesus?"

"Yes, I do," she said with tears forming in her honest eyes.

"Why do you love Him?" I probed deeper.

"Because He died for me."

"Did you invite Him into your heart as Savior and into your life as Lord?"

"Yes, but . . ."

"No buts. Did you?"

"Yes."

"Then, Diane, you are a *truly* born-again Christian."

"But I've sinned since I gave my heart to Jesus. Not only have I sinned, I have been painfully aware of defects in my character that I know God must not like.

Doesn't that prove I'm really not a Christian?"

"Diane, do you long to please Jesus, and do you hate it when you fail?"

"Yes, yes, I love Him, and it so grieves me when I fail."

"You are a true Christian if I've ever met one," I assured her. "And if what you heard at that seminar is true, I've never met a true Christian."

Diane's experience is not unique. The plain Biblical fact is, "We all [that includes you and me] stumble in many things" (James 3:2, NKJV; words in brackets supplied). "If we say that we have no sin, we deceive ourselves, and the truth is not in us" (1 John 1:8). There is no doubt at all that the grace of God is abundantly sufficient to keep us from falling (see Jude 24, 25). The fact that we sometimes fail is no reflection on God's power. It simply means we have allowed our personal weakness to prevail over His power.

The devil would like to get us so focused on our failures that we come to doubt our Christian experience. He lurks in the darkness of discouragement. As the accuser of God's children it is his studied aim to disconnect us from the Savior by stealing our faith and crushing us with despair. Diane's perplexity was really a battle for her soul, a fight of *faith versus doubt*. I can hear her asking, "As I learn to trust God's grace to keep me, how will He relate to me if I fall along the way? Do my failures mean I've never been born-again? Or do I pass from conversion to unconversion when I stumble? Does God reject me at such times?"

1 John 3:9 was quoted to Diane as evidence that a truly born-again Christian is sinless: "Whosoever is born of God doth not commit sin; for His seed remaineth in him: and he cannot sin, because he is

born of God."

A reckless Bible student could easily misunderstand John's intent in this statement. He is not dealing in this Scripture with the occasional misdeeds and failures of the Christian. Rather, he is describing the general direction of the life that has become new in Christ. The Greek verb for sin in this text is in the linear tense, literally meaning sin as an ongoing, unbroken practice. John is not here addressing sin in the punctilious tense, which would indicate an unintentional failure. The idea he intends to communicate is that the born-again believer does not abide in or practice sin as a way of life.

The Amplified Bible gives an enlightening enlargement of this Scripture: "No one born (begotten) of God [deliberately, knowingly, and habitually] practices sin, for God's nature abides in him . . . and he cannot practice sinning because he is born (begotten) of God" (1 John 3:9, The Amplified Bible).

True conversion is a radical change of heart, of motive, of direction. However, the born-again believer is not made miraculously sinless. There are defects of character and weaknesses of the flesh with which he must do battle in the strength of his new faith. As he fights the good fight of faith, he is likely to get knocked down on occasion. His failures will not be willful or intentional, for he loves his Lord and longs to please Him in all things. The steady direction of his new life will be onward and upward. He will sincerely grieve over his mistakes and get up and go forward. "For a just man falleth seven times, and riseth up again" (Proverbs 24:16).

Our standing of justification in Christ is not revoked every time we err. "For the Lord seeth not as man seeth; for man looketh on the outward appearance, but the Lord looketh on the heart" (1 Samuel 16:7). When the genuine desire of the heart is to please and honor God, and faithful efforts are put forth to this end, the Lord Jesus looks on this heart-attitude as the best we can offer. He makes up for our deficiencies with the merits of His own righteousness. In our moments of failure He does not disclaim us as His children. At such times He draws all the closer to persuade us of His unbroken acceptance and deliver us from the clutches of despair. In the words of King David, "The steps of a good man are ordered by the Lord, and He delights in his way. Though he fall, he shall not be utterly cast down, for the Lord upholds him with His hand" (Psalm 37:23, 24, NKJV). Jeremiah proclaimed, "His compassions fail not. They are new every morning" (Lamentations 3:22, 23, NKJV).

There are two vital truths we need to keep in mind in order to go forward without giving up:

1. God's empowering grace is able to keep us from falling into sin.

2. His pardoning grace is unceasingly extended to cover our unseen defects and to lift us up when we fall.

Both are brought to view by the apostle John:

"My little children, these things write I unto you, that ye sin not. And if any man sin, we have an advocate with the Father, Jesus Christ the righteous" (1 John 2:1).

It is the Lord's ultimate purpose that we sin not, but if we do sin, Jesus stands as our Advocate before the Father. He claims us as His redeemed children when we walk and when we fall.

Here John speaks of a specific act of sin as an interruption to the general course of the believer's life. The beloved apostle says, in essence, "These things I write to you that you would not practice sin as a way of life. But if you do sin in a moment of haste or weakness, remember that you have an Advocate with the Father, Jesus Christ the righteous One."

John is not trying to give assurance of ongoing salvation to one who would turn to a course of willful rebellion against God. Rather, he is encouraging those who do continue in Christ that if they fall and yet rise in repentance, Jesus continues to present them as perfect before the Father. Such failures do not separate the believer from God.

There is only one way the believer can forfeit his standing in Christ. He must return to his former life of sin and cease to trust in the Savior. He must cherish sin in his heart. This is what the Bible means when it says, "Your iniquities have separated you from your God; and your sins have hidden His face from you, so that He will not hear" (Isaiah 59:2, NKJV). Isaiah is not here referring to the defects of character or the occasional mistakes of the one who walks with God. Only a willful course of intentional sin can sever the relationship that exists between the believer and his Redeemer. Even then, the separation is the choice of the sinner and not of the Savior; and the One who died to save us stands eager and willing to renew the relationship. "Let the wicked forsake his way, and the unrighteous man his thoughts: and let him return unto the Lord, and He will have mercy upon him; and to our God, for He will abundantly pardon" (Isaiah 55:7).

Never confuse the willful sin of one who has turned from the Lord with the failures and defects of the believer in Christ. As a born-again child of God you can be certain of His power to keep you from sin and you can be assured that He does not cast you away if you fall. Be careful to keep both His power and His pardon in mind. If you emphasize one to the minimizing of the other, you may end up in self-righteousness on the one hand or in despair on the other.

The fact that we need not fall into sin was so over-emphasized in Diane's mind that she became blind to the merciful advocacy of Christ. She lived in constant anxiety that her sins were greater than His grace. On the other hand, there are others who so over-emphasize the fact that God is quick to forgive that they cease to be diligent to partake of His power for victory. They look lightly on sin and presume upon the mercy of God.

Jesus didn't die to excuse sin, but He did die to forgive sin. His forgiveness is always extended with the higher purpose of total victory in view. He does not intend that sinning and forgiveness would be a never ending cycle for His children. He wants us free from sin. As one dear sister said, "Yes, He loves us just the way we are, but He also loves us too much to leave us that way."

Do you love Jesus, dear friend? Do you long to please and honor Him in all things? Do you hate sin and grieve over your failures? If so, you are a truly born-again Christian and the Lord is at your right hand to empower and to pardon as you have need. Lift your head and take up the warrior's chant penned by Micah:

"Rejoice not against me, O mine enemy: when I fall, I shall arise; when I sit in darkness, the Lord shall be a light unto me" (Micah 7:8).

What matters most is that your understanding of God's love allows you to get up and go forward when you have fallen. The problem with the view Diane encountered is that it will hold you down under a burden of guilt. We do not help people rise above the power of sin by telling them that if they fail, God disclaims them as His children. Rather, victory comes as we believe that God is able to keep us from falling and that He is quick to lift us up out of our failures. There is nothing so perfectly calculated to strengthen the heart to overcome sin as the abiding assurance of God's love and acceptance.

Diane, wherever you are, I do hope the assuring light of God's love still shines in your heart. I share these things with you and with others like you so that the power of sin may be broken in your life. But remember, if you do sin, you have a gracious Advocate with the Father—Jesus Christ the righteous One.

Dear Father, thank You that You are powerful enough to keep me from sin and merciful enough to embrace me with pardon when I fall. May I never abuse Your mercy, but ever respond with deepest desire to please You in all things. I am Your child in Christ. Amen.

8

The Judgment

In the Light
of God's Love

"The sinner's only hope is to rely wholly upon Jesus Christ. . . . Our acceptance with God is sure only through His beloved Son, and good works are but the result of the working of His sin-pardoning love. They are no credit to us, and we have nothing accorded to us for our good works by which we may claim a part in the salvation of our souls. Salvation is God's free gift to the believer, given to him for Christ's sake alone. The troubled soul may find peace through faith in Christ. . . . He cannot present his good works as a plea for the salvation of his soul."

Our High Calling, p. 118.

*T*here's more power in a Mazda RX7 than there is in the Church."

You're probably as startled at these rather melancholy words as I was when I first heard them. I take that back. I think I was more startled, because I heard them straight from the mouth of a dead-serious college student who informed me that the only reason he was at my seminar was to gain the required credits. Right on the heels of his bleak assessment he announced his planned *exodus from Adventism.*

"As soon as I'm done with college, I'm done with playing church."

As you might imagine, my deeply convicted Adventist heart was pierced through. Quite frankly, I hardly knew what to say. I mean, this kid had an attitude toward the Church that frighteningly resembled how Axel Rose of *Guns 'n' Roses* feels about police officers.

"So do you mind telling me why you feel the way you do?" I couldn't help but try and probe the source of his feelings.

"Well, everyone's always talking about all the stuff we have to do and all the stuff we better not do or

Eighty-one

God's gonna bring our names up in the judgment and sentence us to hell. And then it's like they all of a sudden remember that there's suppose to be something positive about all this, so they say 'Oh, yea, and don't forget that God loves you.' It's all so contradictory. I don't know how it makes decent sense to anyone."

With the *ValueGenesis Studies* revealing that as many as 70 percent of our young people do, indeed, make their exodus from Adventism, I wonder how many of them would voice similar frustration . . . if they would dare do so?

Did you notice that the young man who shared the above thoughts indicated particular disdain for the doctrine of the judgment? The whole idea was downright depressing to him, and for good reason. Analyze his understanding. You'll quickly see the source of his burned-out attitude.

According to how he has the pieces put together, God is more like Santa Claus than a Savior, only worse. He's got a list and he's checking it *more than twice*, to decide whether we've been naughty or nice. If the naughty deeds out-number the nice, guess what? Not only no presents, but no paradise either. And not only no paradise, but perdition in its place.

In this young man's mind he heard the Lord basically saying, "Here's My list of extremely difficult rules—keep them, perfectly I should add, or else you're doomed."

You know what? If I had that concept of the judgment, I think I'd want to make my exodus from Adventism too. But the truth is, no matter how many people believe that the judgment is God's last ditch effort to make sure as many people as possible are lost, it just is not true.

According to John, the beloved disciple of Jesus, the judgment belongs in the category entitled "The Everlasting Gospel" (see Revelation 14:6, 7). The reason this is so significant is because the word *gospel* means *good news*, or *glad tidings*. It could even be rendered, *happy message*. From a purely Biblical point of view, unmingled with our misconceptions of God's character, the judgment is a truth intended to impart happiness.

So what's so good, glad and happy about being judged by a holy God? Well, like every truth of Scripture, the judgment becomes clear in the light of God's love. I repeat, because it's worth repeating, only in the light of God's love does any part of reality make "decent sense," to borrow my troubled friend's lingo.

Think together with me for a few minutes as we build an understanding of the judgment on the sure foundation of God's love. Let's begin with the Lord's basic intent toward us:

"The Lord is not slack concerning His promise, as some men count slackness; but is longsuffering to usward, not willing that any should perish" (2 Peter 3:9).

"For I know the thoughts that I think toward you, saith the Lord, thoughts of peace, and not of evil, to give you an expected end" (Jeremiah 29:11).

"Who will have all men to be saved, and to come unto the knowledge of the truth" (1 Timothy 2:4).

There has never been a human being, and never will be, for whom God's desire is anything short of eternal life. Because His very nature is love, it would be more impossible for Him to want any person to be lost than it would be for you to want a child of yours to die in the flames of a car crash. Such feelings have not even the slightest place in His infinite heart of perfect love.

Then why will He ever judge anyone? Actually, He won't. That is to say, God the Father won't. He has "committed all judgment unto the Son" (John 5:22). And for very good reason. Notice how Jesus explained why the Father has given Him the responsibility to judge the world:

"For as the Father hath life in Himself; so hath He given to the Son to have life in Himself; and hath given Him authority to execute judgment also, *because* He is the Son of man" (John 5:26, 27).

Did you catch the point? Jesus is our judge by virtue of His humanity, "because He is the Son of man." That ought to seriously alter our thinking about the judgment. Why? Just think about it. One who became our "brother" in the flesh, One who is "touched" with our feelings, One who was "tempted in all points like we are," One who "carried our sorrows and griefs," One who suffered and died for our eternal salvation—it is this One who is our Judge. He has invested His very own nature and life in our salvation.

The real question to ask is not, "How can I possibly make it?", but rather, "How can I lose?" With Jesus on my side, as my Brother and companion in temptation, I can have the total assurance of ultimate victory in the judgment. "Being confident of this very thing, that He who has begun a good work in you will complete it until the day of Jesus Christ" (Philippians 1:6, NKJV).

Yes, there is one way, and *only* one way, you can make yourself a loser in the end. But it won't be because your list of bad deeds is longer than your list of good ones. Compare these two scriptures:

"Ye will not come to Me, that ye might have life" (John 5:40).

"There is therefore now no condemnation to them which are in Christ Jesus, who walk not after the flesh, but after the Spirit" (Romans 8:1).

Do you see? Those who are lost at last will be lost because they refused to come to Jesus, not because He played *hide n' seek* or *hard to get*. Salvation is not something we attain by trying hard enough to be good. Rather it is something we receive because *He* is so very good as to offer it to us before we even know how to be good. We can't earn it, because He's already given it. In Jesus our salvation is an accomplished reality. If we say *yes*, it becomes our personal reality. If we persist in a course that says *no*, we will ultimately judge ourselves unworthy of eternal life. Though it will grieve Him terribly, and though he longs for our redemption with springs of love as deep as eternity, He will honor our choice by concurring with our own judgment.

There is, of course, a brighter option. Those who come to Jesus find in Him eager acceptance with absolutely no condemnation. The judgment for these glad individuals will mean the final declaration of their acquittal before the onlooking universe. For them the judgment really is good news. As Jesus taught, they will not be condemned in the judgment:

"Verily, verily, I say unto you, he that heareth My word, and believeth on Him that sent Me, hath everlasting life, and shall not come into condemnation; but is passed from death unto life" (John 5:24).

Some people believe that Jesus saves them initially by His free grace through faith, but will ultimately expect them to stand on the merits of their obedience in the judgment.

Make no mistake about it, those who come to Jesus are made more than conquerors through Him who loved them. Victory over sin is the ultimate experience of every truly saved child of Christ. But also know that their final pardon in the judgment is as much a gift of free grace as was their initial pardon the day they first came to Jesus as helpless sinners. The plan of salvation is the same yesterday, today and forever . . . and in the judgment. We are saved by grace alone, through faith alone, in Jesus Christ alone, not adding one particle of merit by anything good we have done.

Now I can hear some sincere, law-abiding Adventist saying,

"But wait just a minute. All this sounds good and great, but the Bible clearly teaches that we are going to be judged by and rewarded according to our works. Certainly this proves that our obedience plays a part in our salvation."

It proves no such thing. What it really proves is that God is more gracious than we can ever fully grasp or appreciate.

How so?

While He saves us wholly by His free grace, He will actually reward us as though we had shared in the accomplishment of our salvation and deserved credit for it.

Notice these insightful words:

"Although we have no merit in ourselves, in the great goodness and love of God we are rewarded as if the merit were our own. When we have done all the good we can possibly do, we are still unprofitable servants. We have done only what was our duty. What we have accomplished has been wrought solely through the grace of Christ, and no reward is due to us from God on the ground of our merit. But through the merit of our Savior, every promise that God has made will be fulfilled, and every man will be rewarded according to his deeds" (*Welfare Ministry*, p. 316).

Remember what we learned in chapter four of this book. It is more accurate to say that good works are *inevitable* for the Christian than to say they are *necessary* for salvation. While it is true that we're not saved by obedience to God's law, it is also true that the true Christian *will* be obedient to God's law. We are not saved by good works, but the true Christian life *will* be filled with them. We are not saved by living a victorious lifestyle, but the true Christian *will* live a victorious lifestyle. And because salvation *will* manifests itself by producing holy aspirations and a life honorable to Christ's name, ultimately we are judged by our works, not because they possess merit, but because they bear testimony to our genuine acceptance of His saving grace. Obedience, good works, victory over sin—these are not the means by which we gain salvation, but rather they are the inevitable manifestation of the salvation we have so freely in Christ alone.

The one who has truly encountered and yielded to the love of Christ does not reason, "Well, if I'm saved by grace through faith alone, then I can have the pleasures of sin and eternal life too."

Not at all. A much higher motive than personal gain has taken hold of the heart that has embraced the cross. To the one who has tasted the sweet release of Christ's pardoning love, the purpose of holy living is as clear as the sun at noonday. The honor of God, the glory of Christ—this is the flaming passion that burns brightly in the soul. Yes, it is true that we are saved by his mercy alone, but can you see that in this precious reality itself is all the reason in the world to live . . . and live . . . and live for Him?

Good works for the Christian are not payment, but praise. Obedience for the Christian is not law-keeping, but love. Victory over sin is not mere duty, but shear delight.

Believe it or not, there is something involved in the judgment of far greater importance than our personal salvation. The honor and glory of God's own character is at stake. The judgment is God's way of making His character transparent and His verdicts accountable to all of His intelligent creation.

The fact is, God is omniscient. He knows everything. He knows the contents of every heart. He knows who has truly received Christ as Savior and who has not. The judgment does not provide the Lord with any information He does not already have to aid Him in His sentencing. He does not pour over the record books to gather evidence against us or to find in us something worthy of salvation. He has no questions to which He needs answers. But we do, and so do the angels and the inhabitants of unfallen worlds. It is for our benefit that the record books are kept. It is for our benefit that the judgment will bring to light the true contents of every heart.

Imagine what heaven would be like if God were to try and solve the sin problem without a judgment. Allow me to illustrate.

The great controversy is over. All the saved are in heaven. All the lost have been destroyed. Those who are saved notice that some of their loved ones and friends are not there. It dawns on them that people they cared for are eternally lost. With much anguish and confusion, they turn to the Lord and ask,

"Lord, why is my brother not here? It seems to me that he was an honest, sincere person. I don't understand."

To this the Lord simply replies: "I am God. I know everything. I read every heart. Your brother's sentence is just. You'll just have to take My word for it."

Can you imagine how you would feel at that point? Devastated, I would suggest. But don't be alarmed. God will never give such an empty response to such an important question. The record books of heaven and the judgment will make certain that every crucial question in this awful conflict between good and evil is answered to the satisfaction of all.

The scenario will be more like this:

"Lord, why isn't my brother here?"

"I know it is difficult to accept the loss of those you love. But I want you to know that I did all that could possibly be done to save each one, including your brother. An accurate record was kept of every effort on My part and of every response on his part. Those records were opened in the judgment as countless angels and twenty-four human elders reviewed each case. Now those records and the results of the judgment are open for your review. I am certain you will see that My sentence is just, and I will be eager to dry your tears."

Our first one thousand years in heaven will be primarily devoted to answering our questions concerning the saved and the lost. The judgment will be opened to our investigation. We will have the opportunity to look into the secret history of any life; and we will discern the love and justice of God in each person's destiny.

Only with accurate records and an open-to-all investigative judgment can the sin problem be truly and eternally solved. Only by methods of love can justice be executed to the satisfaction of all intelligent, volitional creatures. And only a God of love would choose to relate to us with such respect and patience.

Praise Him for the judgment! It really is good news.

Father, gracious God, how wise and marvelous are all Your ways! Thank you for building the judgment into the plan of salvation. I really don't need to fear the judgment, for I will not stand under its scrutiny on my own merit, but on the merits of my Savior, Jesus Christ. Eternal pardon will be written by my name, not because I'm good, but because He loved me so much as to lay down His life for my sins. I am joyfully in Christ. Amen.

9

When Trials Come My Way

In the Light of God's Love

❧

"The Father's presence encircled Christ, and nothing befell Him but that which infinite love permitted for the blessing of the world. Here was His source of comfort, and it is for us. He who is imbued with the Spirit of Christ abides in Christ. The blow that is aimed at him falls upon the Savior, who surrounds him with His presence. Whatever comes to him comes from Christ. He has no need to resist evil, for Christ is his defense. Nothing can touch him except by our Lord's permission, and 'all things' that are permitted 'work together for good to them that love God.' Romans 8:28."

Thoughts From the Mount of Blessing, p. 71.

A close relative of mine recently decided to strap her feet in one of those slippery things called a snowboard. Not only did she get on it, she went up a mountain and let gravity have its way with her. She spent most of the day getting up. There were a few moments of . . . I guess they call it *fun.* But the fun was all over after she fell just right (or should I say, *just wrong*) and sprained her wrist. There was pain. There was disappointment. There were tears.

And there was also theology.

After the accident, a well-meaning friend had this question: "Maybe that means God doesn't want you snowboarding."

The implication could be drawn from such a question that God maybe sent an angel or possibly spoke a word to trip the snowboarder as punishment for doing something of which He does not approve. I know God created the law of gravity, and I am certain He did not invent snowboarding. But I also know that God does not trip snowboarders to express His displeasure. Just what He thinks about the sport, I don't know.

It seems this question about God's character lurks

in all of our hearts. Often I have seen it surface in the midst of trial.

A car accident occurs and someone asks, "Where were you going? Maybe God stopped you."

Illness sets in and the sufferer wonders, "Is God punishing me for something?"

Finances are tight, so we begin to think God is perhaps upset about something.

Is this really how God operates? Does He run cars off the road? Does He introduce sickness into the body? Does He drain our bank accounts when we're not looking?

The disciples had a similar question for Jesus about a blind man: "His disciples asked Him, saying, Master, who did sin, this man, or his parents, that he was born blind?" (John 9:2). Read between the lines. Do you hear what these Christians were asking? They didn't want to know *if* God had afflicted this man with blindness. That was a given. Of course the blindness was from God, they assumed. All they wanted to know was whether the man was being punished for his own sin or the sin of his parents.

Jesus gave a surprising answer: "Neither hath this man sinned, nor his parents: but that the works of God should be made manifest in him" (John 9:3). Jesus was not saying that this man and his parents had never sinned, but that his blindness was not a direct punishment from God because of some specific sin. That does not mean that blindness or other tragedies do not sometimes occur as a result of personal sin. The point is, God does not arbitrarily make bad things happen to us in order to vent His anger or stop us in our tracks.

Through the prophet Jeremiah the Lord proclaims,

"I know the thoughts I think toward you, says the Lord, thoughts of peace and not of evil, to give you a future and a hope" (Jeremiah 29:11, NKJV). The problem is, we often don't know God's thoughts toward us. We imagine He has plans to harm us when in reality He only desires our happiness. You can search the infinite heart of God to its deepest depths and you will never find anything but good will . . . for you, for me, for every member of the human family.

Someone is bound to challenge such a view of God as too good to be true.

"Wait a minute, I know God is good, but this sounds a little too good. Surely He doesn't have such a favorable attitude toward everyone, and certainly God has stopped a few people in their tracks by making horrible things happen to them. What about Sodom and Gomorrah and the Flood?"

This is a good question, and it deserves a good answer. Let me attempt to give one. Follow me carefully.

As I have traversed the Holy Scriptures from Genesis to Revelation, four types of ill-fate have surfaced:

1. *The Natural Results of Sin*: Sin has tragic effects. Just like touching a hot stove burns, and jumping off a cliff compresses flesh and bones to the ground, so sin is painful and destructive. "Whatever a man sows, that he will also reap" (Galatians 6:7, NKJV). "The curse causeless shall not come" (Proverbs 26:2). "Sin entered into the world, and death by sin" (Romans 5:12). "To be carnally minded is death" (Romans 8:6). "The way of transgressors is hard" (Proverbs 13:15).

Bad things happen because of sin. Imagine if sin had no painful or destructive effects. Then it would not be an evil force. The problem with sin is that it's wrong, and it's wrong because it hurts us. Sin violates the laws God has designed for our happiness and well-being. If God were to miraculously prevent the destructive results of sin, He would in effect do away with His law and excuse sin. There would be no reason for us to view sin as evil. When the tragic effects of sin are felt, they are just that, the effects of sin, not the will or work of God.

2. *The Result of Violating Natural Law:* Heat burns. Gravity pulls. Pressure explodes. All the natural laws God has set into motion He intends for our blessing. If there was no heat, we would freeze. If there was no gravity we would float away. As much as we complain about the results that follow the breaking of natural laws, we would not want to live without those laws. We would like to be able to fall and not get hurt, but we like even more the fact that gravity holds our feet to the ground when we walk.

Taking the subject of natural law into a diabolical context, we must remember that the devil and evil men do tamper with nature and try to harness its power to suit their destructive agenda. When the war between good and evil is ended, many natural disasters that were attributed to God will be seen to be the work of the evil one.

Improper care of the earth and disrespect of its boundaries produce destructive effects as well. Fires, floods, and earthquakes often cause mass destruction as a result of our careless and foolish ways of pursuing life on this planet. Apart from God's wisdom, we simply do not know what we are doing. And often nature lets us know we are not as smart as we think we are.

God does not want us to get hurt by nature. He would much rather we turn to Him for wisdom and live in obedience to nature's laws. Another option would be for Him to banish all natural law, but we wouldn't be happy with that either.

3. *The Recklessness of Sinners:* Evil people do evil things to innocent people. We call this crime. "The good man is perished out of the earth: and there is none upright among men: they all lie in wait for blood; they hunt every man his brother with a net" (Micah 7:2). "One sinner destroyeth much good" (Ecclesiastes 9:18).

Jesus told the story of the good Samaritan. An innocent man, minding his own business, fell prey to a band of robbers. He was beat and left to die. Two men with no compassion passed him by. A third came by and helped him (see Luke 10:30-37).

Where was God in all of this?

He did not send the thieves to attack the innocent man. Nor did He put it in the hearts of the first two passers-by to leave him for dead. The tragedy was not the will of God. The only part God played in the whole event was to inspire the heart of the third man with compassion.

This is probably the most difficult aspect of human suffering for us to reconcile with the idea of a loving God. Rape. Murder. Child abuse. War. Why doesn't God step in and stop it all? Is it because the Lord is heartless? Is it because He is powerless? No! There is only one reason He allows this sinful world to continue another minute: "The Lord is not slack concerning His promise [to end the nightmare of evil], as some men count slackness; but is longsuffering to usward, not

Ninety-seven

willing that any should perish, but that all should come to repentance. . . . Account that the longsuffering of our Lord is salvation" (2 Peter 3:9, 15; words in brackets supplied).

God's love sees beautiful potential in the vilest sinners. His patience has paid off. Just think of some of the people He has been able to redeem and transform:

Nebuchadnezzar, the ruthless, murderous, haughty king of Babylon. He may be your neighbor in heaven.

Paul, formerly Saul, the cold-hearted persecutor of Christians. Stephen will be surprised to meet Paul on resurrection morning.

And then there is you and me, as worthy of death as anyone else. God waits because He loves. If He had not waited, so many would be lost who could have been saved. In the process of the plan of salvation, He does not agree with, encourage, or in any way orchestrate the terrible things people do to each other. If we only knew His heart, we would find that He wants it all to end more than we do.

4. *The Merciful and Wise Judgments of God:* In Scripture there are clear examples of divine power bringing destructive judgments on wicked men. The annihilation of Sodom and Gomorrah and the Flood are displays of direct divine retribution. It is within the sovereignty of God's authority and within the boundaries of His love to use the forces of nature and the power of His word to execute judgment. According to His own testimony He has done so in the past and He will do so in the future:

"For I will pass through the land of Egypt this night, and will smite all the firstborn in the land of

Egypt, both man and beast; and against all the gods of Egypt I will execute judgment: I am the Lord" (Exodus 12:12).

"And I will punish the world for their evil, and the wicked for their iniquity; and I will cause the arrogancy of the proud to cease, and will lay low the haughtiness of the terrible" (Isaiah 13:11).

In every case, without exception, the divine judgments of former times and those ahead are the exercise of divine wisdom and mercy. Never has God lost emotional control or laid aside the supremacy of His love to get even with His enemies. Never has He caused human suffering for the sake of personal satisfaction. For He says, "As I live, saith the Lord God, I have no pleasure in the death of the wicked; but that the wicked turn from his way and live: turn ye, turn ye from your evil ways; for why will ye die?" (Ezekiel 33:11).

God has never acted contrary to the very best interest of all His created beings. Not once has He violated the reigning principle of His nature, which is love. "His works are perfect, and all His ways are just. A faithful God who does no wrong, upright and just is He" (Deuteronomy 32:4, NIV).

God is not the source of the small daily annoyances that try us, nor is He the cause of the major tragedies that afflict us. But He does possess sovereign power over the affairs of every life, over all of nature, and even over the devil and all his followers. What does this mean at the practical level of our lives? It means that no trying experience, either small or great, ever happens to us that He does not allow for our ultimate benefit.

Here again, as with all of God's ways, His love shines forth as an unconquerable power for good. While the Almighty One does not arbitrarily bring evil upon us, in His infinite wisdom He is able to use the trials of life for our best interest. He knows that if He were to shield us from every annoyance and affliction we would become spiritual weaklings and dwarfs in character.

Paul saw God's power and wisdom operating far above the circumstances of our lives. He "worketh all things after the counsel of His will" (Ephesians 1:11). "All things work together for good to them that love God, to them who are the called according to His purpose" (Romans 8:28). The Lord is actually able to work out everything we experience to a profitable end.

There are a number of potential benefits to be gained from trying experiences. Trials may

• awaken in the heart a greater sense of need for God (see Psalm 50:15; 86:7),

• generate deeper trust in the Lord (see Psalm 9:9, 10; 2 Corinthians 1:8, 9),

• make us strong in character qualities such as patience, faith, and humility (see James 1:2, 3; Romans 5:1-5; Job 23:10),

• grant us the privilege of identifying more closely with the sufferings of Christ (see Romans 8:17; 2 Corinthians 1:5; Philippians 1:29; 3:8, 10; 1 Peter 2:21, 22; 4:13),

• enable us to understand the hardships of others and help them find God in their pain (see 2 Corinthians 1:4; 1 Corinthians 12:26),

• and persuade us more fully of the power of God's love to hold on to us (see Romans 8:31-39).

Only God knows what to allow and what to prevent in every case, for He alone is acquainted with the individual strengths and weaknesses of every heart. "God is faithful, who will not allow you to be tempted beyond what you are able, but with the temptation will also make the way of escape, that you may be able to bear it" (1 Corinthians 10:13, NKJV). We can be absolutely certain that nothing will ever befall us that God does not deem for our good. He will always give us either strength to bear our trials or a way of escape.

In one sense we can say that nothing bad has ever happened to us. Because ultimately, when we reach the eternal shores, we will see God's providence in every chapter of our lives. We will not wish we had been led any other way than how He chose to lead us. It will be seen that a bright and beautiful light of love guided our every step.

Praise You Father, for Your sovereignty in my life. It is so good to know that You are absolutely committed to my happiness and well-being. I am confident You will never do anything inconsistent with Your love. Thank You for allowing just the trials I need to keep me close to You and for averting those I cannot bear. In the worthy name of Jesus I pray. Amen.

10

Relating to My Fellow Sinners

In the Light of God's Love

"He who is unmerciful toward others shows that he himself is not a partaker of God's pardoning grace. In God's forgiveness the heart of the erring one is drawn close to the great heart of infinite Love. The tide of divine compassion flows into the sinner's soul, and from him to the souls of others. The tenderness and mercy that Christ has revealed in His own precious life will be seen in those who become sharers of His grace. . . . The ground of all forgiveness is found in the unmerited love of God, but by our attitude toward others we show whether we have made that love our own."

Christ's Object Lessons, p. 251.

*I*t was a terrible rumor . . . too terrible to repeat. Of course that didn't keep it from being repeated. The way people were talking about it, you just didn't even think to question whether it was true. After all, *if someone said it, it must be true.*

In this rare case, however, at least one person decided to challenge the grapevine. After a little investigation and going to the accused individual with the hear-say, to the relief of many the dreaded rumor was found to be untrue. Not everyone was so happy to discover the man's innocence. In fact, one person was downright disappointed.

"Oh no! Are you sure it's not true? I've told so many people, and if it's not true . . ."

You get the point. This guy was actually hoping a false rumor was true. He regretted the fact that an accused man was found innocent. Those to whom he had whispered the report would find out that he had passed on a false charge. The man he already despised would be justified in their eyes. A little plaque in a friend's bathroom seems applicable: "Keep your words sweet. Someday you may have to eat them."

In this particular situation the rumor was false and the accused party was innocent. This is not always the case, however. Sometimes people do actually do wrong. In fact, it seems to be a regular occurrence for sinners to sin. Even within the household of faith, brothers and sisters frequently err. And though we find it convenient to forget, we too misbehave on occasion. We find it easier, however, to overlook our own faults and magnify the failings of others. The Bible points out a few possible reasons why we may do this:

1. *We condemn in others what we are not willing to face in ourselves.*

Paul warns that condemning others may arise out of a sense of self-condemnation: "You are inexcusable, O man, whoever you are who judge, for in whatever you judge another you condemn yourself; for you who judge practice the same things" (Romans 2:1, NKJV). Then Paul probed deeper into the psychology of this problem. He asked, "Do you think this, O man, you who judge those who practicing such things, and doing the same, that you will escape the judgment of God?" (Romans 2:3, NKJV).

Sometimes we judge others harshly because it somehow gives us an illusionary feeling that we are exalted above them in God's eyes. By condemning others we feel like we're right up there on a par with God. We hope that as we stand beside the Lord and point the finger at the sins of someone else He will fail to notice our sins. It's the ol' create-a-common-enemy approach.

"God, have you noticed what that person is doing? How low, how sad, how terrible! It's wrong, Lord, but be assured, *I* would never do anything like that."

By heaping judgment on others we feel we are

more righteous than they and attempt to lessen our own sense of responsibility to deal faithfully with ourselves. I don't mean to be childish, but I'm reminded of something I once heard a five year old say: "It takes one to know one." Sometimes wisdom proceeds from the mouth of babes.

2. *We condemn others when we fail to understand the power of God's goodness to break the grip of sin.*

After confronting us with the fact that we may condemn others in an effort to escape God's judgment against our own sins, Paul offers another possible reason why we might do this: "Or do you despise the riches of His goodness, forbearance, and longsuffering, not knowing that the goodness of God leads you to repentance" (Romans 2:4, NKJV)?

Did you grasp what Paul says here? If we're not careful we may attempt to employ condemnation as a means to arouse repentance in those who do wrong. By failing to realize that genuine repentance is a heart-level turning from sin in response to God's love, we may naively suppose that we can effect reform in those around us by simply pointing out their sins.

"We just need to tell it like it is and let the chips fall where they may. Sin is sin and you had better stop it."

This kind of approach demonstrates a great lack of understanding concerning human nature. Condemnation almost always solicits self-defense. Most people will naturally respond to censor with resistance. On the other hand, most people naturally tend to respect and admire those by whom they feel loved and accepted, and within that context are receptive to counsel and even reproof. We earn the right to offer correction by earning respect.

Paul is clear. It is the revelation of God's good and loving character that generates repentance in the human heart. When we understand this fundamental reality, we will find ourselves more inclined to uplift the cross of Jesus than to point out sin.

3. *We condemn others when we are blind to our own need for God's mercy.*

This is why it was so easy for the Pharisees to condemn the woman caught in adultery. They didn't realize that her sin was no more sinful than their own. But when Jesus wrote out their transgressions on the ground, they fled away in shame (see John 8:1-11.)

Like the Pharisees, we are often quick to demand the execution of justice because we don't see our own need of mercy. None are so quick to condemn as those who are caught in the snare of spiritual pride, but those who recognize their own soul poverty will be slow to judge others.

So inseparable is God's forgiveness of us from our forgiveness of others that Jesus said, "If you forgive men their trespasses, your heavenly Father will also forgive you. But if you do not forgive men their trespasses, neither will your Father forgive your trespasses" (Matthew 6:14, 15, NKJV).

There is no greater evidence that God's love has penetrated the heart than a willingness to allow His love, through us, to "cover a multitude of sins" in others (1 Peter 4:8, NKJV). Conversely, there is no greater proof that a person is not abiding under the conscious reality of God's forgiveness than a disposition to find and condemn the faults of others. The greatest privilege and responsibility of one who is forgiven is to forgive.

4. *We condemn others when we view salvation as something we earn by doing good.*

They say, *Misery loves company*. I think *they* are right, whoever *they* are. When we obey God's requirement merely out of a sense of obligation in order to be saved, we find no real joy in our religious experience. We do what we have to do because we have to do it, not because we really want to. And, in all honesty, we want others to share the grueling burden we bear.

If I feel obligated, you had better feel obligated too. If I can't do this or that without feeling guilty, you had better not either. If you do, I'll be more than happy to let you know that you're not towing the line.

The Pharisees had this problem. They carried themselves with an atmosphere that reminded everyone that they alone were righteous. They were always defining for others what they should and should not do. Always miserable, but always right.

If we view our relationship with God as a cycle of acceptance and rejection determined by our personal good deeds and bad deeds, it's almost inevitable that we will draw close to people when they succeed and pull back from them when they fail. We will feel uneasy in the presence of sinners and secure in the fellowship of those who play church in our own image.

This is why the Pharisees were so uncomfortable with the fact that Jesus associated closely with sinners. It threatened their concept of God. If Jesus was indeed the Son of God, His true representative, then His acceptance of sinners would mean that their self-righteous show was of no value to Jehovah. It would mean that whatever the purpose of righteous behavior may be, it certainly was not to their credit for salvation.

They would need to find another motive for being good—perhaps love—which would be far too self-crucifying. So instead, they crucified Him.

If anyone has ever understood God's love it was the apostle Paul. To him divine love was not merely a beautiful theory to be admired from a distance like a breathtaking work of art. Jesus did not die on the cross to stimulate our intellects or impress us with His valor. He died to demonstrate God's love so that we might be transformed into its image. In Paul's mind, the love that Christ manifested toward us while we were yet in our sins is to find reflection in the way we relate to our fellow sinner. Notice how he weds these two factors together:

"For the love of Christ constrains us, because we judge thus: that if One died for all, then all died; and He died for all, that those who live should live no longer for themselves, but for Him who died for them and rose again. Therefore, from now on, we regard no one according to the flesh. Even though we have known Christ according to the flesh, yet now we know Him thus no longer. Therefore, if anyone is in Christ, he is a new creation; old things have passed away; behold, all things have become new. Now all things are of God, who has reconciled us to Himself through Jesus Christ, and has given us the ministry of reconciliation, that is, that God was in Christ reconciling the world to Himself, not imputing their trespasses to them, and has committed to us the word of reconciliation" (2 Corinthians 5:14-19, NKJV).

In verses 14 and 15 Paul says we are compelled by the love of Christ because we realize that He died for us. Then in verse 16 he points out that the Savior's amazing love alters the way we relate to other people: "Therefore, from now on, we regard no one according to the flesh," or as the Revised Standard Version says, "We regard no one from a human point of view." In other words, the love of Christ changes the way we see others.

Taking this thought to yet a more practical level, Paul continues by reminding us that the reconciliation of the world was accomplished by a specific attitude on God's part: God reconciled sinners by "not counting men's sins against them" (NIV). And it is by this very same means that we are to carry forth "the ministry of reconciliation."

Once we have turned from our sins and come to Christ, it is natural for us to notice the sins of others. One of the gifts of the Holy Spirit is an acute sense of the difference between right and wrong. While this discernment is needful, it also imposes one of the greatest tests we will face as Christians. Will we maintain the distinction between the sin and the sinner? Will we relate to those who are yet in their sins with the same reconciling attitude that the Savior manifested toward us when we were yet in our sin?

The answer may be yes, or it may be no.

Yes, we will relate to others with mercy if we continue to abide under grace ourselves, maintaining a humble sense of God's mercy exercised toward us.

No, we will not relate to others with mercy if, after having begun in grace, we then try to be made perfect by the works of the law (see Galatians 3:1-3).

Those who try to find acceptance with God by their performance will only grant acceptance to others if their performance seems deserving. This religion, though it professes the name of Jesus, is very much the same as the heathen religions that summon the favor of God by good deeds and provoke His wrath by bad deeds. But we don't serve a heathen deity.

The absolutely astounding thing about the one and only true God is that He approaches this fallen world by "not counting men's sins against them." And, really, isn't that the basic meaning of grace? Rather than treat us as we deserve due to our sin, God treats us as though we had never sinned. Where would we be if we got what we deserve? Quite simply, we wouldn't be. If God had dealt out the wages of sin to Adam and Eve, there would be no human race. That includes you and me. Thank God He does not relate to us according to what we deserve as sinners.

Regardless of one's attitude toward God, whether of faith or rebellion, as a committed Father He surrounds every one of us with an atmosphere of grace as real as the air we breath. Jesus said,

"You have heard that it was said, 'You shall love your neighbor and hate your enemy.' But I say to you, love your enemies, bless those who curse you, do good to those who hate you, and pray for those who spitefully use you and persecute you, that you may be sons of your Father in heaven; for He makes His sun rise on the evil and on the good, and sends rain on the just and on the unjust. For if you love those who love you, what reward have you? Do not even the tax collectors do the same? And if you greet your brethren only, what do you do more than others? Do not even the tax collectors do so? Therefore you shall be perfect, just as your Father in heaven is perfect" (Matthew 5:43-48, NKJV).

What a startling portrayal of God is here presented by Jesus!

It is common, He explains, for us to relate in a positive way to our friends and in a negative way to our enemies. Contrary to the popular way of handling those who cross us, the Great Teacher calls us to love our enemies in order that we may be like our Father in heaven. He makes the sun to rise on both the righteous and the wicked. We, too, should encircle with our love and blessing those who do wrong along with those who do good. Jesus says this is what it means to be perfect as God is—to love like God loves.

Not only does God give love and sunshine to every person, He also "gives light to every man who comes into the world" (John 1:9, NKJV). To every inhabitant of earth God imparts a degree of spiritual enlightenment by which each one may be guided to know of the Creator's existence and sense their need of Him. "He also has planted eternity in men's hearts and minds [a divinely implanted sense of a purpose working through the ages which nothing under the sun but God alone can satisfy]" (Ecclesiastes 3:11, The Amplified Bible).

Since God lavishes undeserved life and light and love on saint and sinner alike, should we not regard one another with at least equal compassion and patience?

When you notice the sins of others, it will be helpful if you remember a few things:

• Before you knew the Lord He did not count your sins against you (see 2 Corinthians 5:19).

• He saved you according to His mercy, not by works of righteousness that you have done (see Titus 3:5).

• No one has ever committed any sin of which you yourself are not capable (see Titus 3:3).

One hundred thirteen

- Your eagerness to condemn sin in another person may be a reflection of your own guilt (see Romans 2:1).

- How would you fare if God were to hold you as accountable for your sins as you hold others accountable for theirs (see Matthew 7:2)?

Those who allow themselves to be embraced by the love of God will embrace others with that same love. They understand that God won them by forgiveness, and by the same means they will seek to win sinners and restore backsliders. In the light of God's love expressed toward us at Calvary, how can we regard others with any less compassion than He has shown us? The goodness of God led us to repentance. Only in the light of His goodness should we expect others to turn from sin to the Savior.

And many will, if we let them.

Lord God, Your mercy is beyond me to fully grasp. It is truly amazing that You have regarded me with such tender compassion. Thank You for not holding my sins against me before I knew You. Please help me to relate to others with the same attitude so they will be drawn to You and not repelled. I pray in the merciful name of Jesus. Amen.

11

How to Experience God's Love

"With untold love our God has loved us, and our love awakens toward Him as we comprehend something of the length and breadth and depth and height of this love that passeth knowledge. By the revelation of the attractive loveliness of Christ, by the knowledge of His love expressed to us while we were yet sinners, the stubborn heart is melted and subdued, and the sinner is transformed and becomes a child of heaven. God does not employ compulsory measures; love is the agent which He uses to expel sin from the heart. By it He changes pride into humility, and enmity and unbelief into love and faith."

Thoughts From the Mount of Blessing, *pp. 76, 77*.

*W*ater flows through riverbeds on its way to lakes and seas. Seed is carried on the gentle breezes and wild whippings of the wind to find its place of germination in the soil. Blood moves through veins and capillaries to reach every organ of the human body. From two-wheelers to eighteen-wheelers, automobiles travel on paved highways to deliver people and goods to their appointed places.

Everything with a destination has its medium of transit and a purpose to accomplish.

God's love is no exception. It has a destination—your inmost heart and mine. It has, as well, a channel of access through which it makes its crucial journey into our hearts—the perceptive faculties of the mind. Having reached our hearts through the medium of perception, divine love has a vital purpose to accomplish—to impart needed strength so we can live a life reflective of its selfless beauty.

The apostle Paul communicated this concept in a powerful prayer he offered for every believer in Christ:

"For this cause I bow my knees unto the Father of our Lord Jesus Christ . . . that He would grant you, according to the riches of His glory, to be strengthened with might by His Spirit in the inner man: that Christ may dwell in your hearts by faith; that ye, being rooted and grounded in love, may be able to comprehend with all saints what is the breadth, and length, and depth, and height; and to know the love of Christ, which passeth knowledge, that ye might be filled with all the fullness of God" (Ephesians 3:14-19).

Paul realized that we have need of a specific kind of strength, the kind that resides on the inside. So he prayed that we would be "strengthened with might by His Spirit *in the inner man*." Isn't that the quality of empowering for which we all so desperately long? Don't we sense our need for a spiritual energy that flows forth from deep within our hearts?

- Inner strength to resist temptation.
- Inner strength to obey God's law.
- Inner strength to share our faith.
- Inner strength to forgive our offenders.

Really, that's the only kind of strength that will prove sufficient in the serious heart-matters of Christianity. Paul yearned that we would have more, much more, than a superficial, surface religious experience. He prayed that our relationship with God would reach down to the motive level of our *inner person*.

To be a good disciplinarian is not equivalent to being a good Christian, even if the code of discipline we follow happens to be the law of God. For "by the deeds of the law there shall no flesh be justified in His sight" (Romans 3:20). There is no degree of law-keeping, no good behavior good enough, no amount of effort sufficient enough to secure for us the release from sin that so often eludes our grasp. For the very moment we pursue salvation by means of the good we do and the evil we refrain from doing, grace is frustrated and we're on our own. "For if righteousness comes through the law, then Christ died in vain" (Galatians 2:21, NKJV).

Such endeavors may make us appear strong in our convictions, but in reality we are secretly weak when we build upon the brittle foundation of self-centered motivation. There are many apparently strong religious people who are actually on the verge of crumbling on the inside. They do what they should do *because they should*, and refrain from doing what they shouldn't do *because they shouldn't*. Period! God's transforming grace hasn't penetrated the outer layers of self-interest. His love is unknown to them, except, of course, as a matter of formal confession. It hasn't penetrated beyond their heads into their hearts. Every act of obedience and every turning away from sin is entered into with one consuming focus—to escape hell and gain heaven. Paul reached far beyond all this in his Ephesians 3 prayer. He petitioned the throne of grace that we would be "strengthened with might by His Spirit *in the inner man*."

In verses 17 through 19, Paul progresses in his prayer to become more specific as to the nature of the inward strength he desires for us. Two times he names our much needed empowering as "*the love of Christ*." Far from a passing thought, throughout Paul's writings God's love, as it was manifested in Christ, is a constantly repeated theme.

In Romans he explains that when we receive the justifying grace of Christ, "the love of God is shed abroad in our hearts" (Romans 5:5). The apostle knows only one source of this love: "God demonstrates His own love toward us, in that while we were still sinners, Christ died for us" (Romans 5:8, NKJV). The cross defines the quality and depth of divine love for unworthy sinners. Concerning the practical effect of God's love in the life of the receiver, Paul claims that "love is the fulfilling of the law" (Romans 13:10).

To the Corinthians Paul wrote, "The love of Christ constraineth us . . . that they which live should not henceforth live unto themselves, but unto Him who died for them, and rose again" (2 Corinthians 5:14, 15). God's love is so powerful that it vanquishes the root cause of all sin, which is selfishness. He declared to those at Corinth the absolute nothingness of religious activity, no matter how apparently good, when not motivated by a heart filled with divine love (see 1 Corinthians 13:1-3).

Addressing the works oriented Galatians, Paul sought to banish from their minds any hope of obtaining God's favor by virtue of self-motivated works, only to introduce to them a Christ-centered "faith which worketh by love" (Galatians 5:6). Not that works are of no importance at all, but to this cross-preaching apostle faith, is the paramount issue, and good works are the product of a love-motivated faith.

He called the Ephesians to be "holy and without blame before Him [the Lord] in love" (Ephesians 1:4). He went on to explain that God saved us because He is "rich in mercy, for His great love wherewith He loved us" (Ephesians 2:4). In the wake of this almost unbelievable love, Paul envisioned a Christianity wholly governed by its self-abandoning influence. He even developed a list of the areas of life that will be positively affected as we abide in the light of God's love:

- We are to relate to "one another in love" (4:2).
- We are to speak "the truth in love" (4:15).
- We are to edify the church "in love" (4:16).
- We are to "walk in love, as Christ also hath loved us" (5:2).
- We are to conduct our marriages in love (5:25).

We could go on to highlight the same emphasis in Paul's other epistles and letters. At the heart of all he preached we find the central theme of *God's love poured out through Christ.* If the great apostle were alive today and we could ask him for a one sentence summary of his message, he might say something like this:

Through the cross of Christ God demonstrated His matchless love toward us in order to move and empower us to cease living for ourselves and to live for His glory in conscious response to His love. (Adapted from Romans 5:8 and 2 Corinthians 5:14, 15.)

The practical question must arise, "How are we to receive into our hearts and experience in our daily living the power of God's love?" Until we answer this vital question, all our talk about the love of God is just that—mere talk. The Lord intends that His love be far more to us than an emotionally stimulating idea. He wants it to be an experiential reality for us, to touch every aspect of our lives with healing, overcoming power.

But how? Let's get practical.

In Paul's Ephesians 3 prayer we find an extremely clear answer to our question. Three times, with different words, he makes known the medium through which we may receive God's love. In verse 17 he prayed that we would be "*rooted and grounded* in love." In verse 18 he pleads that we would be able to "*comprehend*" God's love. In verse 19 he asks that we would "*know* the love of Christ."

According to Paul, God's love seeks entrance into our hearts through the medium of comprehension. He believed that the perceptive faculties of the mind must be aroused to understand the singular quality and true greatness of divine love in order for its benefits to be realized. He expected, as a result, that previously untapped moral power would spring forth to shape and govern our practical lives.

This is precisely why Paul was so passionate in his determination to preach "Jesus Christ, and Him crucified" (1 Corinthians 2:2). He had come to sense and appreciate the self-abandoning love manifested at the cross and was held its willing captive. "The life which I now live in the flesh," he exclaimed, "I live by faith in the Son of God, who loved me and gave Himself for me" (Galatians 2:20, NKJV). To this one who had previously hated Jesus and persecuted His followers, there was no power so powerful, no influence so influential, no attraction so attractive as the Son of God willingly hanging upon the cross under the curse of sin so that we who nailed Him there might have eternal life.

I imagine Paul telling himself before each sermon he preached, "If they can only be led to comprehend the love of God in Christ, surely they will not be able to withhold their hearts from Him." Then as he stood before his hearers he would strive to articulate, in the clearest, most persuasive words he could muster, the ineffable love of his Savior. The tremendous success of Paul's ministry bears testimony to the unrivaled power of God's love to move and change the self-centered hearts of men and women.

To *comprehend* the love of Christ is to apprehend its significance with the mind. There is another word in Paul's vocabulary that makes the comprehension of divine love an active pursuit for the believer. That word is *beholding*. Notice how he uses it in 2 Corinthians 3:18:

"But we all, with open face beholding as in a glass the glory of the Lord, are changed into the same image from glory to glory, even as by the Spirit of the Lord."

Beholding is the deliberate action of the mind to focus, meditate, or dwell upon a matter in order to gain a clear understanding of it. By beholding the character of God as demonstrated in Christ, the truly personal application of His love will dawn upon the heart. New aspects of divine mercy will shine forth. Deep impressions of God's love and goodness will be made upon the mind, calling to life feelings of gratitude and adoration that will transcend the power of selfishness. As we grasp the character of God's love and come to appreciate its unreserved outpouring toward us, a motive-cleansing miracle will occur. Living for God in unswerving obedience to His law will no longer be seen as a confining duty performed to gain heaven, but as a liberating privilege for God's glory.

We could break down the formula like this:

- Beholding (or focusing upon) the cross produces comprehension of God's love.
- Comprehension of God's love awakens gratitude in the heart.
- Gratitude creates responsive love.
- And love willingly and eagerly obeys God's will.

We put so much energy into focusing on our sins and trying to overcome them to the neglect of the one spiritual discipline that would make our efforts successful—to behold the true character of God as manifested in Christ. If we would but turn our eyes upon Jesus, and look full in His wonderful face, the things we struggle to let go of would grow strangely dim.

I used to wonder at our spiritual weakness as a people. Now I'm not amazed at all. The reason is clear. We've preached doctrinal truth. We've preached prophetic truth. We've preached the necessity of obedience to God's law. But we have put Jesus and His cross after the comma in almost a whisper.

THE SEVENTH DAY IS THE SABBATH, NOT SUNDAY, we exclaim, and oh yeah, Jesus died for you.

THE DEAD ARE REALLY DEAD, NOT ALIVE, and Jesus loves you.

GOD'S LAW IS STILL BINDING AND SHOULD BE OBEYED, and Jesus will help you.

We have communicated loud, but not real clear. Let's try it Paul's way, with an exclamation point after Jesus Christ and Him crucified.

JESUS DIED FOR YOU, EVEN YOU, BEFORE YOU EVEN SENSED YOUR NEED OF A SAVIOR! And you will be pleased to know He has given us the Sabbath to remind us of our total dependence on Him. So rest in faith that He will complete the work He has begun in your heart.

JESUS LOVES YOU WITH A LOVE SO VOID OF SELF-INTEREST THAT HE WILLINGLY SUFFERED THE GUILT OF YOUR SIN SO YOU CAN BE FREE! And, by the way, death is but a sweet sleep in the assurance of His mighty power to raise you at His coming.

IF YOU ALLOW HIS LOVE TO ENTER YOUR HEART, IT WILL TRANSFORM YOUR MOTIVE FOR LIVING FROM SELFISHNESS TO LOVE! Then his law will become your delight and you will find power to obey in the strength of His love.

The world awaits "the truth *as it is in Jesus*." But we can't give it to them until we have it ourselves. It is my sincere prayer and the urgent purpose of these pages that we would sense the power God has invested in the cross. May we find the true significance of each doctrine we hold in the beautiful light of God's matchless love. Amen.